# 50 Words for *Love* in Swedish

# 50 Words
# for *Love*
# in Swedish

A memoir in fragments of a foreign language

**Stephen Keeler**

archetype books

First published in Great Britain in 2021 by Archetype Books.

A CIP record of this book is available from the British Library.

ISBN 978-1-9997637-4-9

Printed and bound in Great Britain by Clays Ltd, Elcograf S.p.A.

Set in Chaparral Pro, 10.5/14pt and Fira Sans 10/13

Author photograph on page 159 by Rob McDougall, for Scottish Book Trust.

Archetype Books
Clarendon House, 52 Cornmarket Street, Oxford, OX1 3HJ
archetypebooks.net

FSC
www.fsc.org
MIX
Paper from
responsible sources
FSC® C018072

Archetype Books is committed to supporting local economies and businesses with genuine concern for the environment. This book is printed on paper from responsible sources. Clays, our UK printer, is ISO14001 compliant, using 100% renewable electricity and recycling 98% of their waste.

For my wonderful daughter, Lucy,
and in memory of Yvonne Marie Keeler
(1950-2003)

Paradise for the disappearing objects and everyday diversions of the past might simply exist in being remembered and mentioned.

Maria Stepanova
*In Memory of Memory*
(translated by Sasha Dugdale)
Fitzcarraldo Editions, 2021

# Contents

# Part 1

I qualified as a teacher in the early summer of 1973, but in the months before that I had begun to be aware of a growing dread. The thought of a designated threadbare chair in the staffroom of a 1960s and therefore bleak comprehensive school in a former Durham mining town filled me with unease. I didn't want to become an even angrier young man than I already was, bitching about 3B's *Lord of the Flies* essays through clouds of Embassy cigarette smoke at break; becoming cynical, sarcastic and much too old much too young. I didn't want a sports jacket with leather elbow patches. I didn't want to have to fumble around with the only other probationary teacher on the staff and end up marrying her in Barnard Castle or Chester-le-Street or Yarm, with a crippling mortgage and a used Hillman Imp and something living inside me eating it all away. I had read *Room at the Top*, and it had done the trick.

While my peers began to study the appointments pages of the *Times Educational Supplement* with a fervour we had rarely demonstrated in our academic studies – some of them even making wedding plans at the same time – I was racked with a melancholy restlessness. The last three years were already becoming nostalgia, and, having no obvious way of prolonging them, I was suddenly fired with the urge to escape. I am not sure I analysed too much what it was I thought I was escaping from: modern poverty, the over-sentimentality of the north-east of England, my home town, my mother, two outgrown 'relationships', a dull prospective marriage, the authority of what we then readily (and inaccurately) called The State Education System; the mundane, the familiar, the despised?

The only page of the *Times Educational Supplement* I looked at was the Overseas Appointments page. Actually, I only ever looked at it once, spotted entirely by chance an advertisement for a teaching post in Sweden, applied, was twice interviewed, appointed, briefed and duly transported from Gatwick to the newly built Arlanda Airport, then an optimistic hour or so from Stockholm by bus, today a quarter of that by non-stop express train. Until that moment I had not set foot on foreign soil. Until I got the job I'm not sure I could readily have found Sweden on the map. Nothing in my life to date had prepared me for the direction it was about to take.

I arrived in Sweden later that summer with a teaching job and a small rented cottage by the church in Mariestad. It was my first time out of the UK, and it might have been anywhere: my only motivation was just to get out; to leave the dark and drizzly northern town of my birth, the solemn cloisters of my alma mater, and to avoid at all costs the perhaps imagined horrors of an English school staffroom.

I spoke sub-schoolbook French, minimal German and no Swedish, and yet in Stockholm I found a city which seemed to have been waiting patiently for me to arrive. In Mariestad I found a pretty town of quiet, jolly people all of whom seemed pleased that I had come. If only life were like that!

Well, for me, in Sweden, it was, and I have spent the rest of my life reciprocating. As the poet said, you only fall in love for the first time once. It is neither over-dramatic nor an exaggeration to say that everything I am I owe to Sweden in general and to a number of individual Swedes in particular.

Mariestad sits on the shores of Vänern, in the green and

relatively temperate province of Västergötland. Vänern is the largest lake in Scandinavia and sits like a huge, lop-sided medallion on the slender chain that is the Göta Canal linking Stockholm on the east coast to Gothenburg on the west. I rented a small wooden cottage with an apple tree in the garden, within easy reach of its still waters. It was like something straight out of the Carl Larsson paintings I had yet to discover.

My address was in Kyrkogatan, next to the cathedral, *domkyrka*, which is evidently not a cathedral (no bishop), in the inverted-U-shaped Old Town where the floury bakery still had a golden *kringla* figure-of-eight biscuit hanging over the door, and tiny angled mirrors were attached outside the drawing-room windows of the bourgeois residences so that those inside could observe passers-by without being seen. All very Strindbergian and, to the gauche young man-not-man I was at that time, somewhat stultifying.

Unlike its slenderer neighbour to the east, Lake Vättern, famous for its immodest pink water lilies and the moody and bouldersome forests made famous by John Bauer which surround it, Vänern is still a working lake. There are sawmills and paper mills, ceramics factories, engine plants and small boatyards in the handful of larger towns dotted around it, and raw materials for some of the remaining heavy industries to the west still pass silently and distant across it, like shifting, reflective shadows.

The first word I learned in Swedish was *mask ros*, which means 'dandelion'. I know it has to be impossible for that statement to be true, in the normal sense of the word 'true', but memory seems to order according to its own priorities, which are not always susceptible to human logic or constructs of veracity.

I learned the word, or strictly speaking the two words, *mask ros*, several months after moving to the small town of Mariestad, on the shores of Lake Vänern, in the late summer of 1973, and it cannot be that I communicated solely in English until then, or that this particular lexical item would have proved to be of much immediate practical use once learned.

No, I must have known the words for stamps and post-cards, for bread and milk and for the transactions involved in buying train tickets, travelling by bus, paying my rent. *Mask ros*, however, always suggests itself as the first word I learned in what was to become my limited but deep-rooted vocabulary of love.

My first winter in Sweden had seen the threat of Oil Crisis petrol rationing, *ransonering* – surely a stronger contender for first-word status since it was never out of the news during those nervous months in which my characterisation of Swedishness began to formulate, began to fix. That Christmas I had returned briefly to Britain, to my native north-east England, laden with Swedish candles and a cheese slice for everyone. It was years, however, before I learned to call a cheese slice an *osthyvel*. So *mask ros* it is.

1
_____

## **bageri** *bakery*

baːgerʼiː

It is from childhood rhymes and games and toys that
we take our first notions of how society is ordered, its
functions and offices. The candlestick-maker may have
come along only for the rhyme, but the butcher and the
baker – or Mr Bun, if you prefer – still maintain a place
in the scheme of things.

I walked past Hutchison's cake shop at least twice on
every one of my school days over more than a dozen
years, in the dark and drizzly northern town of my
birth. Mrs Hutchison seemed made of different stuff
from the lumpen, suffering women who brought me up.
Quietly cheerful, always with a smile for me and forever
tucking back a wisp of curly hair into the baker's
bonnet she wore at work, she had a husband, Seth, a
giant of a man in thick white overalls, floury apron and
floppy white cap, whose domain was the cavernous but
silent bakery behind their shop. There was an invisible
but somehow always present daughter, Deirdre, of
whom great things were whispered after polite enquiry.
Is this where my fascination with bakeries germinated,

behind glass counters and wooden trays and silver cake stands and doilies?

The *'Kringlan'* Bakery was just along the street where I lived in Mariestad. I had to pass it to go anywhere, and I soon acquired a small vocabulary of bread just by looking in the steamed-up window as I passed – *limpa*, a loaf or bap, of rye or wholewheat bread, *fullkorn*, wholemeal, and *bulle*, bun. In season, I learned *lussekatter* – the saffron-flavoured, 'S'-shaped buns made at Lucia and *semlor* – the cardamom-flavoured bread buns filled with marzipan and whipped cream and only available during Lent.

At Furudals Bruks Kursinternat, where I was an occasional language tutor for almost twenty years, there was a bakery. Furudals Bruk was derelict in parts when Lennart Öhnell and his wife Inger started to buy up bits of it during the early 1970s. Their vision was of a village for enlightened education. They bought or leased the old schoolhouse, which became the office and conference room, the manor house, *herrgården*, for accommodation and a dining room; the brewery, *brygghuset*, for classrooms, and the bakery, *bageriet*, over which they built a modest bungalow as a resident tutor's accommodation. Over the next thirty years, they bought or leased or borrowed all the buildings that made up the village and built Furudals Bruks Kursinternat into a successful and sprawling enterprise and I'd love to tell you more but this is not the place for its history. I was blessed to have known it and to have worked there in its golden age.

The Bakery was where Maj-Britt and Gun would bake the Bruk's bread and its legendary crispbread, *knäckebröd*, and where I learned that the best bit of crispbread is the bit you don't normally get – the disc they cut out of the centre so that the baked crispbread roundels can be stacked or hung on wooden poles. That middle bit – and maybe it's like cheese – always tastes nuttier, crisper and lighter than any other part. Now for thick butter, thin cheese, and since we're next to the manor house it may as well be *Herrgårds Ost* (literal translation: 'manor-house cheese'), and a generous dollop of Swedish marmalade: *smaklig måltid!*

2
___

## **Ballograf** *a brand of pen*

bʌlɔgr'ɑːf

I decided I'd write the first draft of this manuscript with a grainy, slightly scratchy Ballograf ballpoint pen, and I am instantly back in Sweden, filling in one of those flimsy, carbon-impregnated deposit slips they used to have at the post office, when Sweden still had a Post Office. The pens there, and in every bank, library, town hall and government office, were always Ballograf – the only pen made in Sweden.

Like the gorgeous Ericsson Cobrafon I had in my first Stockholm apartment, and the chubby Saab 92, the Ballograf 'Epoca P' is a Swedish design classic. All my students – all of them – had Ballografs. Always. Most were black or white or grey. Today there's a dynamic and delicious range of colours and the Ballograf is making a retro comeback.

As a gauche young man from 1960s England, I simply wasn't able to comprehend the absence of choice as policy. If you design a product for use and manufacture it to a high standard, where is the need for choice? It is an argument. I was still wedded to something close to a belief that there somehow *ought* to be twenty different toothpastes on the supermarket shelves.

My daughter and I still buy each other Ballografs
for Christmas and birthdays, even though neither of
us uses a pen very much. For her, I think, they are a
small homage. For me, an instant bridge back to grey,
high-ceilinged classrooms on snowy winter nights in
provincial towns across the country, where diligent
students called Siv and Sigrid and Kjell scribbled in
vocabulary notebooks. The old king was still alive, and
ABBA had yet to imagine 'Waterloo'.

## 3

# **bastu** *sauna*

'bʌstu

A sauna is not a sauna in Swedish. 'Sauna' is the Finnish word. The Swedes call it *bastu* – a conflation of *bad*, bath, and *stuga*, hut or cabin.

I had my first sauna at the municipal swimming pool in a small town in Sweden in the early 1970s. I had been invited by a Swedish colleague who turned up with his wife and their three young children, all of whom tumbled naked into the sauna together.

I had been briefly instructed in the procedures and etiquette of the sauna and was convinced I was about to undergo trial by extreme ordeal. But as I sat in the muted pinewood light, as hot and as naked as the dozen or so others of all ages and body shapes quietly baking together, it came to me as an epiphany that this was sublime.

I was still an idiot British kid from the north. I had been nowhere. I knew nothing and couldn't even get by yet in the gentle language being exchanged around me. Someone offered me a beer. Two of the children wanted me to go on the water-slide with them. My colleague smiled. The scene was lit for a painting by an Old Master.

I bought the house where I live now in the Scottish Highlands because it had a sauna, but before this Yvonne and I had lived quietly and comfortably in a south-west London suburb for almost thirty years. Towards the end of the 1980s our over-the-road neighbours installed a sauna and for a decade they would switch it on of a Sunday afternoon, and I was always invited. I would cross the road carrying two fat towels and half a dozen bottles of chilled Czech beer, and a couple of hours later I would cross back again, having set the world to rights with B and J, to read my daughter Lucy a bedtime story, then spend a quiet evening while Yvonne did a pile of marking and prepared her lessons for the coming week.

Here, in this house I bought for its *bastu*, I have an elegant, lozenge-shaped enamel sign on the door to mine: black, cursive lettering on pale grey – *Bastu*. Pale grey like the rest of the 'Swedish wall' I created in the hall, with its faux eighteenth-century dado, moulded skirting boards and wood panelling. The modern fakewood door has been clad with panels to resemble doors in the manor house, *herrgården*, of Furudals Bruk where I worked for almost twenty years. And the *bastu* sign itself?

I had known at the outset that buying my Scottish home with a sauna would entail a trip to Stockholm for an enamel sign.

It was a mild, late summer afternoon, in 2011. Stockholm was drowsy as a wasp in a window. The huddles of tourists were heading back to their hotels, and the streets of the Old Town were quiet in the lengthening shadows.

Lucy and I found the shop easily enough and I was delighted to spot exactly the the sign I wanted, pinned to a small board. I expressed my delight and my gratitude that this Stockholm institution was still in business after all these years, and quite probably I said that I had made the journey from northern Scotland just for this 50-kronor (about £5.00) sign.

We talked, the proprietors and Lucy and I, and then we talked some more. Occasional customers came and went, and still we talked, of Stockholm in the 1960s and 70s, of England which they loved, of my late wife, of Lucy's young hopes and enthusiasms, and of our new house in the Scottish Highlands with its sauna and the small sign that would soon be nailed to its door.

Breathless with our enthusiasms and the goodwill of the day, we seemed suddenly aware of a sense of an ending. Nothing lasts for long. It was time to close the shop. Lucy was hungry. I wanted a drink. The man shuffled behind the counter. The woman disappeared behind a curtain at the back of the shop. Lights were turned off as I paid for my little sign and we turned to go.

'Just a moment...' It was the woman. She was writing something on a thick sheet of cream paper. She rolled it with care and tied it with ribbon.

'Take this with you and enjoy it in your new home.'

Yvonne Zedell is a painter. She and her son run an art and antiques shop in the Old Town, Gamla Stan, in Stockholm. They also make and sell bespoke enamel signs for gates and mailboxes and rooms in the house – *Se Upp för Hunden*, Beware of the Dog; *Köket*, The Kitchen; *Toalett*, Toilet; yes and *Bastu*, if you want one.

Yvonne Zedell's charming watercolour is now the centrepiece of my Swedish wall, next to the belle époque mirror and the framed photographs of Orrefors glass designs from the 1920s. It is a painting I could look at for hours, and sometimes do. It is called *Vinterresa till jul*, 'Winter Journey to Christmas', and shows Zedell's son as a young father with his family about to board the handsome ferry, *Storskär*, to spend Christmas out in the archipelago. The painting glows with fondness and ease. He is carrying a large straw *julbock*, the Christmas goat that helps Santa deliver presents, and there are packages and parcels, backpacks, suitcases, scarves and sturdy boots. There's a beagle on a lead watching two hooded crows on the quayside. The wife's red coat is the same red you see in the paintings of Carl Larsson and Anders Zorn; the low, snow-filled sky, the gouts of steam from the funnel, the iced quayside. And along the bottom, in tiny, elegant handwriting, the pencilled dedication, 'To beautiful Lucy & Stephen from Yvonne'. It was my late wife's name, too.

## 4

___

# **bio** *cinema*

'biːɔ

On a freezing Sunday afternoon in the late autumn of 1973, the wind chill suggesting minus ten, I realised I was already acquiring the Swedes' obsession with the temperature. I'd come in from the cold to sit in the gloriously outdated *Bio Wiktoria*, Victoria Cinema, in Mariestad, having by now learned enough Swedish to get me a ticket in the back stalls and a bar of Marabou chocolate.

There was no doubt I was the only Englishman there for the matinée, but I was by no means the only foreigner. The tiny shell-like cinema with its art deco pretensions was packed with dozens of doctors and teachers, pharmacists, accountants and members of the numerous professions and trades which had so enraged the then president of Uganda, Idi Amin, that he had expelled them from the country in their thousands and at short notice the previous December. Sweden invited 800 Ugandan Asians to come and live there, and most were relocated to Mariestad.

As Erich Korngold's magnificent theme inflated the auditorium like a bouncy castle and Errol Flynn seemed to fly across the screen in Lincoln green, we must have been the most improbable sight in Sweden that Sunday afternoon: a tiny urban cinema yearning to be Grauman's, filled to the back circle with well-dressed but shivering Ugandan Asians, a gormless Englishman, a couple of dozen local teenagers no longer needing the subtitles and perhaps expecting privacy, and a handful of elderly couples who must have started having doubts about their grasp on reality as they looked around them for something familiar. *The Adventures of Robin Hood*, starring Errol Flynn and the divine being that was the young Olivia de Havilland, has ever since been my favourite feel-good movie. I have never since failed to fall in love with any woman called Olivia.

Yes, to the Anglocentric eye it looks more like the word for detergent than for a movie theatre, but *bio*, a shortening of *biograf*, especially when 'written' in neon script and embedded in those gentle wooden shop-front signs once ubiquitous across Sweden, will forever trigger a Korngold Sunday afternoon, chilled in the old sense of the word but warmed with a flush of (not entirely innocent) nostalgia.

# 5

## björk *birch*

bɪ'ərk

Nothing is quite so Swedish as the silver birch. North-western Russians, Karelian Finns, Estonians and even the odd Icelandic musician might disagree, but nothing says Sweden more than the 'forest eyes' of its bark and the immodest shimmer of its newly opened leaves tied around the village *majstång*, maypole, at *Midsommar*.

If Karin Bergöö, wife of the painter Carl Larsson (1853-1919), and arguably a more accomplished artist, created the Swedish interior design style now known around the world courtesy of IKEA, her husband can be said to have iconicised the birch tree as a symbol of Sweden.

The paintings of Anders Zorn (1860-1920) are sumptuous with *gran*, dark spruce. John Bauer (1882-1918) loved the romance of slender *furu*, brooding pines, but Larsson lit his outdoor domestic scenes with the reflected white of the silver birch.

Folke F, a friend of Yvonne, was the consummate forester. He could drive his old Volvo soundlessly on gravel roads. I once saw him kill a mink with a single pebble from a slingshot at near-as-dammit a hundred metres. We had little in common and I sometimes wondered how far his friendship extended, but he was generous beyond reason. His *lingonsaft*, whortleberry/ lingon cordial, was incomparable; his *fläderblomsaft*, which we'll come to, almost as good as my good friend Kerstin's, and often the subject of lengthy negotiations with security and passport control staff at Arlanda airport since he would never let me leave Sweden without at least five litres 'for Yvonne'. He was handy with a knife, and made us several beautiful plaited birch-bark baskets, just like something out of Carl Larsson.

And there was a magnificent old birch by the *herrgården* at Furudals Bruk, where I worked over a twenty-year period, which inspired this poem from *They Spoke No English – Eighteen Poems Out of Sweden*, published by Nine Pens Press, 2021.

### After an August Wedding
*For Lennart and Inger Öhnell*

There are birch seeds on the window-sill.
A few have drifted to the table
where I mistook them for
my visitors' carelessness
with the sugar placed for coffee.
They are the flakes of summer
caught in the net curtain
like an atom of mould
held between the terrace chairs
in the vicious webs of angry spiders
they pepper the ink-caps
fade on the pond
they are lost in the gravel
like trampled confetti
after an August wedding.

# 6

## Björn Borg

*the greatest tennis player in history*

bjɜːrn ˈbɔrj

Dear Björn,

I wonder whether you still get fan mail. There must have been a time when it was delivered daily in articulated trucks.

I didn't want to bother you then, but you were just what I needed at exactly the time I needed it in 1976, when I had returned to England after almost four years in Sweden. I was homesick and no one around me in London in those days knew much about Sweden, so there was little sympathy and less understanding.

I had watched you in TV pictures so grainy they could have been from the Moon and I had marvelled at the balletic precision with which you whipped a ball and placed it deep in the corner, impossible to reach. And now that I was living in London, I realised I might get to see you do it in person. A little bit of 'home'.

Back then, Wimbledon had a delightful institution known as 'free standing'. If you queued early enough and were near the front when they opened the gates, and if you ran like hell once you were in the ground, you could get a standing place on Centre Court for the whole day, for the cost of entry – 50p! Imagine that.

And that's what we did, in 1976, 1977, 1978, 1979 and 1980. We saw you, my wife Yvonne and I, win five consecutive Wimbledon championships, almost within touching distance. To this day, in that egocentric way in which we create our superstitions, I think it's my fault you didn't also win in 1981.

It was the first time I couldn't be there. That summer I was working for the British Council in the charming Czech town of Česke Budejovice (world-class beer and world-class pencils), and I had to sit around a TV that sultry Saturday afternoon with colleagues – none of whom could pronounce your name properly – and watch, knowing that because I wasn't there in SW19 shouting *Heja Sverige!*, Come on, Sweden!, *Heja Björn!*, Come on, Björn!, you would lose. And, of course, you did.

Twenty years later I sat on a high bar stool next to you in a restaurant in Grev Turegatan in Stockholm. You were slim and tanned with that floppy grey hair that looks like it costs a million dollars. You wore the most elegant double-breasted suit I have ever seen close up, pale grey and with a silk tie of spun gold. And I so wanted to interrupt your lunch with friends and tell you all this, politely, calmly, and not at all weirdly.

Just that week, I had been up in Dalarna running a workshop for English teachers from your old high school, Blombacka. The week had been punctuated with their affectionate stories of you as a kid, only really interested in reading comics and knocking a ball against a concrete wall. It was a privileged insight. And then, a day later, I find myself sitting next you in a smart restaurant.

I still feel I owe you an apology for 1981.

## 7

## **dagens rätt** *dish of the day*

'da:gens 'ræt

I arrived in Sweden straight from university, where I'd lived in halls for three years and never had to feed myself. I had the basic skills but very little culinary knowledge. The galley kitchen in my Mariestad cottage had a lugubrious hotplate and an uninspiring oven, and when I could be bothered I'd have a go at something out of Katharine Whitehorn's *Cooking in a Bedsitter*. But living alone so young in a foreign country, preoccupied with the new, the strange and the lovely, and with a proper job, a social life of sorts and very little money, I took frequent refuge in and nourishment from the *dagens rätt* at the EPA supermarket on the town square.

EPA – now long gone – had a bright if characterless cafeteria overlooking the municipal bus stops, and daily for five *kronor*, Swedish crowns – equivalent to 50p today – they offered a cooked lunch with a plate of shredded cabbage salad, a slice of crispbread with low-fat butter, and a glass of milk. Charmless but cheap, and fine so long as you didn't mind there being no choice.

The *dagens rätt* had an echo of the social democratic institution about it: a no-frills daily meal for office workers and bank clerks, for pensioners and the lonely.

I grew very fond of *lövbiff,* thin beef 'steaks', and thick gravy, and of the hot pea soup they served on Thursdays. The occasional gristly chunks of pork in it were less delightful, but the pancakes served afterwards with *lingon sylt,* lingonberry jam, which we'll come to, and whipped cream were an improvement on the sugar and lemon juice I was used to once a year in England.

*Dagens rätt* was little better than a school dinner, but it was cheap and I had neither to cook it nor to wash up afterwards. It was, too, a useful introduction to the tastes of proletarian Sweden. The delights of fine dining at Riche or Operakällaren in Stockholm had to wait another decade or more, until we could afford it. But before then, Lennart Öhnell would treat us to a weekend dinner at *Restaurang Anna,* Anna's Restaurant, in Rättvik after we had worked another intensive week at Furudals Bruk, and my friend Birgitta's *Janssons Frestelse,* Jansson's Temptation, was always there for me should I care to drop by. I can't pretend to have enjoyed the *dagens rätt* the way you might enjoy an *omelette aux fine herbes* on the Champs-Élysées or a plate of scallops half an hour out of the sea at home in Scotland, but it fed me the way my fretting mother would have wanted, and would have recognised as wholesome and good enough: *lagom,* in fact.

8
_____

# dill *dill*

dɪl

The smell of dill is the smell of Sweden, when the smell of Sweden is not of pine resin or sawn timber or the dusty long grass of late summer down by the lake. The smell of dill is the smell of all my Swedish friends' kitchens, when it's not flour or freshly baked *knäckebröd* or *sill*, pickled herring. And very specifically, the smell of dill is the ambient aroma of Åhléns food hall.

Åhléns' flagship Stockholm department store and the nearby public space, Sergels Torg, were newly built and incomplete when I first lived there. A shiny new city of glass and steel and concrete was nudging aside the dowager respectability and prim fustiness of eighteenth- and nineteenth-century city centre apartment houses. The Social Democrats' dream was nowhere better realised than in the great ocean liner of a building just down the road from Åhléns: *Kulturhuset*, where anyone could sit all day in the library (and we often did in those penniless days), with books in every language and newspapers from around the world. You could listen to records, look at art, go to the theatre or have an egg-and-prawn sandwich, topped with mayonnaise and a sprig of dill, in the café.

No one attended evening classes on a Friday, so
Yvonne, my soon-to-be-wife, and I quickly fell into
the habit of doing our food shopping then, often after
seeing the seven o'clock movie at the new *Filmhuset*,
our university of cinema on Valhallavägen.

To ride the escalator down to Åhléns food hall late on
a Friday evening was to wade into gentle ocean surf by
moonlight. It was brine and salt and ice; it was Baltic
herring and prawns and dark red crayfish; and it was
*gravad lax* dressed with great clumps of fresh dill.

Wherever in the world I have lived and travelled, the
smell of dill caught entirely out of the blue transports
me back to Sweden in an instant, to Åsa's mother's
meatballs sprinkled with it, to Birgitta's new potatoes
with dill cream sauce, or in downtown Stockholm
just wandering the aisles in the basement at Åhléns,
breathing deep and long and slow.

9
___

### **Felix** *Swedish food brand*

'feliks

I was recently describing my university accommodation
(1970-3) to a friend. I lived outside Durham in a former
army camp that had been bought by my college and
fitted out as student accommodation. There were, I
think, fourteen 'bungalows', each with two double and
three single bedrooms. Another bungalow served as
the communal dining room and common room, and
one more as accommodation for a resident tutor's
family. Decades ahead of their time, my college had
hired a Swedish firm to design and fit out the student
rooms. There were huge fitted wardrobes with sliding
doors, interior shelving and a full-length lower shelf
for shoes and boots and muddy kit. There were fitted
bed frames and an enormous desk with spaces for
pens, typewriters and over-arching Anglepoise lamps.
Everything was made of light-coloured wood, with
leather chair backs and an aluminium wash basin. The
Habitat catalogue had only recently become a thing. I
ordered a dhurry and a 'continental quilt' and – I have
only just realised this – I was living in Sweden (or at
the very least a Swedish environment) before I ever
considered looking for that first overseas post. I have
since wondered to what extent my departure to Sweden
three years later was mere coincidence?

On my first visits to a supermarket – EPA – I came across the Felix brand: *rödbeta*, pickled, crinkle-cut beetroot; *gurka*, sliced pickled cucumber; *bruna bönor*, brown beans in a sweet tomato sauce to be eaten with salty bacon *kötbullar* meatballs; and ketchup in an iconic squeezy long-neck bottle – squirted over macaroni, it became a staple for my first year in Mariestad (together with *kokt korv*, which we'll also come to). I was living the dream.

I have, since my student days, grown fascinated by trace memory. Its magnetic and liminal almost-non-existence is the poet's greatest resource. Even writing 'magnetic', for instance, sets off a silent screening in muted colours of two plastic dolls, male and female, less than 10cm tall (though it would have been four inches in those days), with delicately pivoted heads. As a very young child I must have seen them placed opposite each other on a table, then pushed gently forwards by an adult finger until they 'kissed', drawn together by a small magnet inside each doll's head. Real or imagined, and if imagined, any less real? And whether real or imagined nonetheless endowed with the power to affect.

Real or imagined, the bigger-than-me cardboard cut-out of a cartoon cat in the window of Binns' food hall, in Blackwellgate, Darlington, circa 1956, has stayed with me these more than sixty years. It had a moving part, a red tongue which licked its lips in appreciation of the Heinz tomato soup it was there to advertise. For over sixty years I have never passed that window (long gone, in fact) without looking to see whether Felix the Cat is still there, has returned, or was actually never there.

A decade or so on, Yvonne and I were living in south-west London, pregnant. We decided that if we had a girl she'd be Lucy Astrid (after the children's author Astrid Lindgren) and if it was a boy he'd be Felix Magnus (after our good friend Carl-Magnus Annell).

Our child was a girl, and I'm delighted she loves her second name. Had she been a boy, well, I wonder about Felix, and why breakfast is never really complete for me without *knäckebröd*, thin slices of *Västerbottens Öst* cheese, and Felix sweet pickled *gurka*.

## ___ 10

## **fläderblomssaft** *elderflower cordial*
'flæ:dərblʊms'sʌft

It is a small act of love to pronounce this word.

Because Swedish is a foreign language to me,
there is an intensified precision in my attempted
pronunciations of it. It is the intensity of a lover. *Flä /
der / bloms / saft*. I love what the word makes me do
with my lips and tongue. I am reminded of Sondheim's
'Maria'. And because it's a word, and especially perhaps
because it's a noun, it has image. And where the beauty
of the word on the page comes together with the
performance of its pronunciation and the dreamlike
image, you have another word for love. Say it soft
and it's almost like being on that cold, wind-whipped
Öresund beach looking across to Denmark, long before
'The Bridge'.

I was in Sweden with a photographer friend to produce
a schoolbook about the life of a 'typical' Swedish
girl, Sara. We were staying with Sara's family, in their
handsome suburban home in Vellinge, just outside
Malmö. Dad (Karl-Magnus – how about that for a grand
Swedish name), a newspaper editor, was a runner. He
took me on long, exhilarating runs, races really, among
the pollarded willows and the wind turbines. Sara and
older brother Fredrik never seemed to get bored with
our requests for posed photographs doing things they

almost never did. And Mum, Kerstin, a schoolteacher, made *fläderblomssaft*.

The book was done, we had all the photos we needed and it was our last afternoon before driving north to Gothenburg to take the ferry back to England. The week had been unseasonably warm and bright but on our final day the clouds had gathered and the wind had picked up, but nothing to prevent a family of hardy Swedes from going ahead with the trip to the beach they'd promised us.

I have a photograph here. We are wearing all the clothes we had with us. Even the children are bloated with padded jackets and mittens. Karl-Magnus stands in the dunes like a conquering Viking. Kerstin's laughter has a touch of reserve at the corners of her mouth. Sara found specks of amber on the beach, and I, as so often in Sweden looking in from the outside, could not believe how unfeasibly kind life was being to me.

As we drove back to the handsome suburban home, the clouds rolled over onto Denmark and the sun shone down on Sweden. My photographer friend cooked dinner for the family that evening, as a thank you for their hospitality, and by the time it was ready it was warm enough again to sit out on the terrace. *Fläderblomssaft* was proposed as an appetizer, and a large jug appeared from which generous measures of this vaguely urine-coloured liquid were poured. If this were a movie I'd want us to drift into a dream sequence now. Cue the harps.

Neither sour nor over-sweet, with the faintest suggestion of the tree from which the flowers had come. It is difficult to avoid cliché because it really was as though a hundred summers among the wildflower hedgerows on this gentle coast were distilled into a precious liquid, so much more than a mere beverage. Without a trace of alcohol in it, it was the most intoxicating drink I have ever taken.

Of course we took Kerstin's recipe, and of course we never made it. How could the grubby elderflowers we gathered under Heathrow flight-paths, along the A316 or by Hampton Water Works in Surrey and Middlesex ever hope to invoke the amber beaches of the Öresund, or bittersweet, long-grass Bergman summers?

Stephen Keeler

# Part 2

In 1970s, social democratic, welfare state Sweden, it was neither wise nor common to be an aristocrat. Deference was officially discouraged, 'position' despised, 'status' distrusted. Class, as a social issue, was passé. Sweden was, at least on the surface, politically correct a quarter of a century ahead of the rest of Europe. This was, although I did not know it then, the decade of Per Wahlöö and Maj Sjöwall, whose police procedural crime novels were an open critique of the country of (former Prime Minister) Tage Erlander's 'Boys'. It was the time of Astrid Lindgren's *Pomperipossa* – an attack, in the form of a satirical children's story, on Sweden's punitive tax system that had Lindgren herself paying 103% income tax for a while. *Pomperipossa* was a piece of writing that rocked the Swedish government, if not the State, and almost brought down the then Finance Minister, Gunnar Sträng.

In sleepy, prosperous Mariestad, however, some things were slow to change.

I worked for an extra-mural offshoot of an extra-mural offshoot of Stockholm University, teaching English in schools, factories and the public library and at evening classes. Once a week I would buy a *biljet, tur-och-retur*, return ticket, to Laxå, a comfortable, small and sprawling town an hour north through the forest in a charming waddling railbus painted orange and cream and with polished wooden interior coachwork. Once there, I would teach an afternoon class at the high school, then an evening class, stay the night in a small pension whose owners were unfeasibly welcoming, have cheese and sweet marmalade for *frukost*, breakfast, the next day and then return to Mariestad.

Most of my students were adults. English was obligatory at school and the majority of Swedes I met between the ages of nine and, say, thirty spoke English well enough to communicate without difficulty. In those days, most Swedes over thirty spoke German, and many of those who came to my lessons were middle-aged to elderly folk with an excellent command of German but relatively little English. One such group comprised a dozen or so ladies of a certain age. They were genteel, well-educated, had travelled widely in Europe, married well and – most of them – survived successful and wealthy husbands to become delightful and wealthy widows.

Their children had been educated at quietly excellent universities and now ran national newspapers or major state industrial concerns. These ladies, all but one of them, lived in substantial villas or elegant nineteenth-century apartment buildings and drove discreet, ageing Mercedes, an occasional Saab or, rarely, a Volvo. Their clothes were for the most part English, expensive and unremarkable except for the quality of the tweed, the cut of the tailoring and the generosity of the lining.

They were a delight to teach, though in reality I taught them nothing. They taught me more than I can quantify.

The exception to the suburban villas and nineteenth-century apartment buildings was the house of someone to whom all the others deferred. She had, though she didn't use it, an aristocratic title – a *von* – in her surname, and she lived in a splendid yellow residence, spread out like butter over a small estate, with stables and horses, just out of town. She was not, I think, a widow. She reminded me of Marlene Dietrich (perhaps it was the *von*), though there was also something of Honor Blackman as Pussy Galore in *Goldfinger* about her, too. She wore thin polo-neck sweaters, jodhpurs and riding boots – or did I imagine all that? Anyway, she was wealthy, charming, seemed to be exceptionally at ease in the world, and although genteel there was about her the suggestion of the possibility of something delightfully outrageous. For this ungainly, daft, ill-kempt northern lad from nowhere, from where women over forty were old and ill and lumpen, and wore shapeless coats and colourless mufflers and cracked and down-at-heel shoes, this was a revelation. It was also an affirmation. I began to know that I had come to the right place. Dull it might be, for now (it could never have occurred to me then that the dullness was *in* me not around me), and I could not then have described myself as happy, but I never for a moment felt I had made a mistake. And in writing that last line it suddenly occurs to me that this was the first and only time in my life that I didn't want to be somewhere else.

Stephen Keeler

# 11

## frukost *breakfast*
'frukɔst

The delightful, kind and entirely silent couple who ran the pension in Laxå where Börje Stern arranged for me to stay on Wednesday nights always brought me breakfast on a tray with an embroidered cloth and a wooden knife.

I remember it as their sunny living room into which they shoved a single bed for the night for me. There was a fat tin alarm clock like one of those chrome headlights perched on the front wings of ancient cars. Soviet-made, it had a Sputnik on the second hand, jerking out the seconds until morning. I never found a way to silence its monumental ticking no matter where in the room I stuffed it, occasionally forgetting to put it back in place before I left. It was always there again beside the bed each week. I wonder, did they think I was engaged in an esoteric game of fetch, as though I were some alien family dog?

I have always liked the name Gunilla. I have had several students called Gunilla, and briefly a girlfriend. It seems to have gone out of fashion, as names do. Trace memory again: could it be that Gunilla is close enough to 'vanilla' and its elemental snuggling associations with childhood, or might it be that the first tub of *marmelad*, marmalade, I bought was Gunilla brand, or both?

Gunilla marmalade was thin and sweet and neon-bright – none of which is a recommendation – but it came in a cardboard tub with a squeaky cardboard lid, and packaging has always been at least half the appeal of everything I've ever bought, from Dinky Toys to Paul Smith socks. Then I discovered that Swedes like to spread it *on top* of cheese, on crispbread. Try it before you judge. A hard, sharp-tasting cheese is best. Nothing beats *Västerbottens Öst* cheese, to my taste, although *Herrgårds Ost* will do. And a sweeter marmalade than you might normally prefer. Don't spare the salty butter, and if you can get hold of a superior artisan crispbread, so much the better. Marmalade on cheese is Sweden's contribution to the perfect breakfast. With Gevalia coffee. And it never fails to remind me of that bright front room, its potted plants and family portraits; its lace curtains and its little ornaments; of always-sunny mornings in a prosperous little town with a UFO-shaped water tower, far away in the forest.

## 12

# **glassögon** *glasses*

'frukɔst

The literal nature of some of my words for love in Swedish made them an irritant to the idiot boy I was, yet gives them such simple charm now.

A dictionary, *ordbok*, is a 'word book'; *husvagn*, a caravan, a 'house wagon', and a *brysthållare*, bra, is a 'breast holder'. No need to make it complicated when a *sjukhus*, hospital, can be a 'sick house', and the *simhall*, public baths, a 'swim hall'. The one that won my heart, that I use at home, and sometimes in its pidgin English literal translation 'glass eyes', is *glassögon*, often spotted suspended under the wide-eyed pince-nez shop sign still seen outside some opticians in Sweden.

# 13

## glögg *warm spiced/mulled wine*
gləg

Foreign language learning would be so much easier if every word did what *glögg* does: a drink that sounds like what you do when you pour or swallow it.

But does anyone actually like *glögg* after the first one, each Christmas? Or is it more about the imagery?

I had *glögg* on my first Lucia in Mariestad, an occasion I will soon describe, so there are images of shadows cast by candlelight, of warm wood and conviviality. I drank it at my students' Christmas parties in their comfortable homes where shy blond children were allowed to stay up late to see the foreign teacher and giggle. We made our own – and never got it quite right. And we drank it, Yvonne and I, at the *julmarknad*, Christmas market, in the Old Town, our first Christmas in Stockholm.

There was snow, of course there was snow. Our breath clouded as we spoke, steaming up her glasses. We sipped and took great care not to choke on the two blanched almonds at the bottom of the little cup. We warmed our hands on it and moved around the miniature streets of small log cabins selling reindeer meat and pancakes and snow globes and hot dogs and hand-carved wooden decorations for the tree. I have it here, the decoration we bought that night:

hand-painted red and cut with a jigsaw, it is a sleigh
piled high with coloured parcels and is driven by
a top-hatted father with a child beside him on the
seat, the horses prancing like statuary. It is just a few
centimetres long and utterly charming. It cost 3 *kronor*,
crowns – equivalent to 30p then – and has found its
place on every Christmas tree we've had since.

## 14

## herrgården *manor house*

'herg'ɔːrden

I have often remarked on how objects seem to bring
their origins with them, like memory, wherever they go,
wherever we place them. Often this is charming, and it
is what we acquire them for. My Gustavsberg ceramic
eider duck sits in front of me on a woven table-runner
decorated with a lingonberry design by Ekelunds, and
it calms me with its serenity and the softness of its
contours, the images it brings of sunlight among reeds.

Not everything I have brought home from a life of
ceaseless international travel has cast its charm here:
the Portuguese tiles are crude and harsh now; the
French filigree looks only tatty; the German *stein* is
brutal among my other drinking vessels. The Swedish
crystal brought back for an ageing mother, the
birchbark baskets for friends in the north, the poster
for a nephew into science fiction, all refused to settle
here, to shine; to accommodate themselves in British
homes.

When I bought this house, in homage to the
*herrgården* at Furudals Bruks, I drew up a design and
got a couple of local joiners to make me a Swedish
wall. There is a mitred, ogee skirting board below
tongue-and-groove panels and a dado rail. The door-
frame is widened and the door has three moulded

panels, in the middle of which is my enamel *bastu* sign, nailed with handmade Swedish nails. It is painted in the palest of pale greys and has a white-painted wooden plant table in front of it – very Karin Larsson. There's my trident candle-holder made by Matts Fällman, the resident blacksmith at Furudals Bruk, and there's the belle époque mirror on the wall next to an old map of Stockholm, a couple of framed photographs of Orrefors glass designs from the nineteenth century, my Yvonne Zeddell watercolour and a delightful pen-and-ink drawing, *Girl in the Window Opposite,* sent by an old friend and former student of mine, Karin Ahl-Feltzin. There are ten carved wooden Dalarna horses from different parts of that province, a Nittsjö Pottery mug, and a couple of small table mats made by Jobs, the fabric designers near Leksand. A small homage. A little bit of Sweden here in the Scottish Highlands. Continuity of a kind. A way of holding on, if not to a manorial lifestyle then just to life itself for a little bit longer.

I bought it for its plate glass, steel and slate; for its state-of-the-art construction. I bought it, I guess, because moving here was the next best thing to returning to live in Sweden. But despite its high ceilings, tall windows and vast openness – or perhaps because of those things – I knew it needed hinterland, and I knew at once how I was going to make it.

At Furudals Bruks Kursinternat, we tutors were accommodated in the *herrgården* – a late seventeenth-century three-storey manor house built of wood on huge stone foundations. After the years of neglect and its reincarnation as part of Lennart Öhnell's enlightened education centre, the manor still managed to retain a little of its French-influenced interior styling and its up-in-the-forest grandeur. My room, for example, was decorated with a hand-painted frieze of not-quite-cute cherubs, and a cheap reproduction of Anders Zorn's (1860-1920) voluptuous *Margit* with its characteristic use of rich red and fiery orange and its obvious fondness for the artist's model.

Waking each morning to Margit tying up her great red tresses under the frolicsome cherubs had its effect. Over those years, too, I absorbed the high skirtings and moulded panels; the broad doors, heavy rim locks and huge, elaborate keys; the massive hinges and crystal chandeliers; the architraves, the fancy door-knobs, the trompe-l'œil.

A little theatricality was called for up here in the Highlands.

## 15

## ja, juste *yes, exactly*

ˈjaː ˈʃyst

I cannot claim to speak Swedish. I could not, for example, express the subtle difference between that sentence and *Jag tala inte Svenska*, 'I can't speak Swedish.' Sure, I can order an *öl*, beer, even *en stor stark*, a large, strong beer; I can buy a train ticket; and I know how to respond when a shop assistant asks whether I'd like a bag or not. I know appropriate greetings for when I pass a fellow early-morning runner and I can follow the instructions in a municipal car park. But I could not participate in idle speculation about what Björn and Britt might have paid for their new flagpole or what to do about the litter left by visitors at the local lakeside beauty spot. Depending on the subject, I might be able to follow small talk, and I can get the gist of a Scandi noir TV thriller without having to read every line of the English subtitles. But I cannot claim to *speak* Swedish, even though that is the impression I might often, unwittingly, give.

Apart from having 'an ear' for the sounds of languages, and in the case of Swedish a love of making those sounds myself, I early on acquired, without any conscious effort, the catch-all positive response to practically anything anyone says to you: *ja, juste*, yes, exactly; yes, right.

In the same way I acquired English, my mother tongue – by being immersed in it and listening – I acquired *ja, juste*. I similarly acquired the Swedes' habit of taking a sudden in-breath, sometimes without even speaking, to express assent. And once I'd picked up *faktiskt*, in fact, actually, my basic disguise was complete, and I had set up the potential awkwardness that has forever followed: if your pronunciation is pretty good, and you have a feel for stress and melody and can then drop informal idiomatic words and expressions into your otherwise feeble attempts at conversation, *faktiskt* everyone will think you're fluent and will speak at you at an alarming rate, incomprehensibly and with the full expectation you are following every word. I am lucky if there's a pause with rising intonation for an anticipated agreement, for then I can help the 'conversation' on its way with a deftly dropped, *ja, juste*.

## 16

## Kalles Kaviar *fish roe paste*

ˈkʌles ˈkʌvɪʌr

The boy on the patriotic blue tube with yellow lettering has not aged since the day in 1954 when he first appeared. Blond, blue-eyed and freckled, he is the personification of happiness and good health. He is the Swedish equivalent of those wholesome children on the lids of my childhood Bayko sets and in Ladybird Books illustrations and the advertisements for Norvic Kiltie shoes.

His perfect, gleaming teeth are about to bite into a buttered slice of *knäckebröd* liberally laced with Kalles Kaviar. The message is simple and strong: this Swedish, no-nonsense food is not only good for you, it also makes you happy. And how social democratic to call this most proletarian of food products 'caviar': Kalles fish roe paste – caviar for the masses!

Unappealing to look at, surgical pink and with a whiff of Copydex about it in a down wind, this 'caviar' is a surprisingly convivial accompaniment to hard-boiled eggs, sliced on a bed of mayonnaise and garnished with a sprig of dill.

Half a century after I first tasted it and winced, I am now always delighted to find that my daughter has slipped a tube into my Christmas stocking. Which leads me to a theory – that no one has ever fallen fully in love with Sweden who didn't first develop at least an affection for Kalles Kaviar.

## 17

## konditori *coffee shop, tea room*
'kɔndɪtɔ'ri:

Until today, making sure of my translations, I had never come across the compound inelegance of *förfriskningsetablissemang*, literally a 'refreshment establishment'. I might have drunk rather less of the boiled and often bitter coffee available at the altogether more pronounceable *konditori* had I had to learn the longer, clumsier word.

I say available, rather than served, because in a *konditori* once you have ordered your particular *bakelse*, pastry or cake, or *smörgås*, sandwich, usually open, you help yourself to coffee from a jug or kettle, topped up frequently and sitting on a hotplate. It is a defining feature of the *konditori* that once you have bought your first coffee, you can refill your cup as often as you like without further payment.

But it was never the coffee, free or otherwise, that drew me into my first Swedish coffee shops, nor the often fusty fox-fur-and-mothballs air of their murky rooms with tiny tables. Before I gave my heart to *prinsesstårta*, princess cake, forever, before my seasonal infidelities with the *semla*, Lenten bun, and long before I developed a bit of a thing for the *punsch-roll*, a liqueur-flavoured marzipan and chocolate 'pastry', my first love, my formative adolescent affair, was with the *mazarin*, an almond tart in a vanilla-flavoured shortbread case, topped with white icing.

For Proust, it was the sensation of a tea-dunked madeleine that triggered childhood memory; for me, removing a *mazarin* from its waxen case is enough to invite reverie. The coffee sits cooling in thin porcelain. There are lace half-curtains on a brass rod, cheap paper napkins. The sun is low and blinding through streaked plate glass. I read the painted name of this establishment on the front window, in reverse. There are passers-by, the scrape of boots, a lumbering bus churning fresh slush, seeming to shiver. I bring the *mazarin* to my lips and break the icing with my teeth, breathing in the mother's milk vanilla essence, and the cake gives way and crumbles in my mouth. I might even utter an 'Mmm...' out loud. One of my students, sitting unobserved by me across the room, mistakes my little ecstasy for an invitation and comes to join me. She is P of the high-neck sweaters and the golden bob and steel-rimmed glasses, and she is smiling and asking me questions about the weekend and would I like to come to the country despite the snow. The snow I still recall, biting into a *mazarin*: the shivering and the grit and the blinding light of it after fifty winters have come and gone, and P might even now, as I write these words, be standing in her Swedish kitchen teaching her great grandchildren how to bake *mazarin*.

# 18

## korv *hot dog*

kɔrv

It was an easy word to acquire, perhaps because when picked up in metal tongs these floppy, long 'hot dog' sausages always seemed to *curve?*

There was a *korv* stand in the bottom right-hand corner of the *stadstorg*, town square, in Mariestad. Silver and shining and clean. It's where I first experienced Sybylla, the processed meat brand, and began to grow my semi-addiction to these pink, chewy and altogether doubtful meat products. They were gorgeous. None of the slimy, grease-saturated onions (which you could still taste a week later), of my north-of-England heritage, although the pudgy, damp bread finger they were placed in was not unfamiliar.

'*Senap och ketchup?*', asked so quickly it sounded like a compound noun. And yes, always yes to *senap*, sweet mustard. But you could have *korv med mos*, with mashed potato, or *pommes frites*, thin chips, in a little waxed paper tray with a wooden spoonfork, to eat in the street.

Many was the freezing winter evening in 1973-4 when I trudged home to my snug little cottage, stopping on the way for an indigestion-inducing *kokt*, boiled, *korv med bröd*, with bread, *senap och ketchup,* for one

Swedish *krona* (about 10p back then). *En grillad*, a grilled *korv*, *med gurka*, with pickled cucumber relish, was one crown, twenty *öre*.

I don't really eat meat nowadays. Not a vegetarian, I just don't choose meat. But I've never made a visit to Sweden yet when I haven't been tempted by a *korv* stand, somewhere. Like cheap music and pungent cologne, there is something nostalgic about it, something that brings back the early 70s for me, a hopeless optimist in a modest country that had a gentle, faint but discernible smile on its face.

## 19

### **kurbits** *an artistic style*

'kurbɪts

I had assumed that the cabinet was an heirloom, of too much sentimental value to discard, too grim to have in the living room, and so it had been put to use as a store cupboard in the shop at the course centre where I taught.

It was only after I had seen my up-from-Stockholm students, many of them wealthy and knowledgeable about such things, admiring its 'Dala blue' paint and the fine brushstrokes of its decorative motifs that I took more notice of it. I began to distinguish a word often repeated in their comments on the cupboard.

*Kurbits* baffles me still. Botanical and biblical in its origins, it describes both the individual design motifs of stylised gourds and leaves, painted almost Chinese-style with broad brushes, and the folkloric artistic style once popular in the Swedish province of Dalarna (sometimes called Dalecarlia in English).

You see an echo of the brushwork on the tourist-dollar-earning Dalarna horses, still today.

I have always found the trunks and chests and wardrobes painted in the kurbits style both suffocating and strangely depressing. That blue worries me; those motifs have no aesthetic appeal. But the word intrigues, with its biblical echoes of 'cubits' and the little half-trill of the tongue you have to make if you're to pronounce it properly. To a native speaker of English, it suggests a plural, and the '-bits' bit echoes the feeble, cheesy jokes we made when we discovered Sweden had a bubblegum called Sor-Bits.

## 20

**legitimation** *proof of identity*

legɪtɪmʌ'ʃuːn

You couldn't get far in 1970s Sweden without *legitimation*. Withdrawing cash from my Swedish Post Office account, booking an international phone call at the local exchange, buying a couple of bottles of beer, all required me to show my *legitimation*. Easy enough for Swedes, who acquired a lifelong unique *personnummer*, personal identification number, soon after birth or on registration with the tax authorities, but being British, and having non-tax-payer status for my first year there, I had no such number or photographic ID card (this was a time when British driving licences were still tiny, photo-free, linen-backed, stitched booklets).

At first I tried explaining, barely concealing my sense of superiority, that in the UK we had no ID cards or personal numbers, declarations that were met with blank stares. A number was needed. Swedes are generally fastidious in following rules. Exceptions sit uneasily. I began to carry my passport and took some foolish pleasure in shop assistants' discomfort as they tried to fit 'Brit pass' and its serial number into the space on an invoice or receipt designed only to accommodate my non-existent *personnummer*.

My background had not prepared me for this. An Englishman's word, and all that. How naive it seems today, but also how pompous. It took me far too long to recognise that if you want to live in Rome, or Sweden, it might be wise to start doing as the locals do: be less abrasive, less arrogant. Secretly – and of course I didn't recognise this at the time – I resented these daily reminders of my otherness. I already wanted to belong here, and I especially wanted one of the lovely gold ID necklaces all my young students wore. And like so many who want inclusion, I kicked and flounced and declared my opposition to the big brother state on specious grounds of personal liberty and, yes, exceptionalism. Look where that's got us, us Brits.

Sweden was gentle with me, resigned to waiting till I saw my foolishness and arrogance. Or I could just leave and stop bothering them. And it's easy to interpret that as smugness. But I doubt the British state would have been any more enlightened. I am grateful. I finally got my *personnummer*, and free health care, long before Sweden joined the EU in 1995. I never did get one of those lovely gold ID tags. Too late: a gold medallion on a man of my age? Probably not.

# Part 3

L was a member of my afternoon ladies' class. Despite all her careful efforts at discretion it was clear that everyone else in the group, even the relatively young bank under-manager who might have been expected to have rather more social democratic leanings, deferred to her with a kind of fond admiration, a respect that I found both disarming and immensely attractive. The class was scheduled to meet weekly in a not unpleasant room in the basement of the public library. It soon became clear, however, that these ladies were not the stuff of municipal facilities, however impressive those facilities might be to someone like me. My own welfare state would have struggled to provide anything close to the luxury of upholstered, ergonomic chairs, oak tables, flip-charts (and pens), Tandberg tape recorders and overhead projectors, all as standard.

It was soon suggested, therefore, that we meet in the ladies' homes on a weekly roster basis, and it was made clear that I was not expected to demur. My job was to turn up on time with a lesson prepared, and to attempt to teach it. It was also made clear to me, without anyone ever having to say so, that this was at least as much a social occasion as it was an educational one. Any attempt I might make to force my lesson plan on the class against the natural direction the conversation might take would be regarded as not quite civilised behaviour. Somehow, I had the good sense not to object. The weeks and months that followed, through my first long, dark Swedish winter, were illuminated by these jewelled afternoons of what the ladies insisted on calling 'English' tea in Swedish Rörstrand china cups with matching tea plates on which were served slices of the most exquisite home-baked sponges and pastries I had ever seen, let alone tasted. Each of these ladies, even the relatively young bank under-manager, had complete sets of everything, matching, in exquisite good taste and of the highest quality. We used cake forks from the family silver, teaspoons from Austria, and German conserve spoons (they knew all the vocabulary too). There was Swedish honey, English jam, Finnish chocolate and home-made waffles. Their homes were filled with polished house-plants and fresh flowers, their walls crammed with heavy-framed, dark oil paintings – often Swedish landscapes, sometimes family portraits – and I cannot believe that there was not a considerable degree of determined competition between the ladies at least to match each other's hospitality. That would have been the Swedish way: to equal each other, not to attempt to outdo each other. *Lagom* in all things – but that is a word we will return to later.

I remember little of the lessons. The ladies always brought their course books, their adequate notepads and Ballograf pens and propelling pencils with a small eraser on the end. Each had the same dutiful edition of a Prisma pocket *englesk-svensk-engelsk* dictionary, *ordbok*, and I don't recall any of them ever being crass enough to forget to do their homework. They would begin by perching on the edge of their substantial armchairs or sofas – these were pre-IKEA days even in Sweden – like a parody of diligent 1960s typing-pool secretaries about to take shorthand, and I would be momentarily unnerved. Then I'd start the lesson, sometimes with a review of the previous week's new vocabulary or with a quick spelling test or a gap-fill grammar exercise, and I might even get as far as a read-through of one of the topical set texts from the book. But that was usually as far as the ladies would indulge me. There was no text, set or otherwise, that could not be used as a pretext for one of them to launch into an earnest critique of the munici-pal council and its new one-way system around the *centrum*. That might lead to a reminiscence about learning to drive, or the day (not many years earlier) that Sweden had switched to 'right-hand traffic'. Someone would recall learning to ride a bike on a farm in Småland, before the war. Someone else would bemoan the current fashion for mopeds among the (too) young, and this might veer off towards concern for individual and social responsibility, and into what became, in all but name, philosophical debates on the nature of Society: sometimes quite heavy stuff; always what they wanted to talk about. They would check with me from time to time that they had used the correct tense, an appropriate idiom, the right word. My job was to let them talk, to make an occasional contri-bution, and to correct their English. I could not have formulated a more enlightened manifesto for language education.

# 21

## **lektor** *qualified academic teacher*
'lek'tɔr

The advertisement in the *Times Educational Supplement* was for an English *lektor*. There was an Iron Curtain resonance to the word. Only a few years earlier I had sat in the dark Regal Cinema in Darlington watching Sean Connery snatch a Soviet 'Lektor' decoding machine in *From Russia With Love*.

Had the British Centre's advert been for 'teachers', I might have passed it by and ended up elsewhere, another person altogether, a different character in a different story. But no, I was going to be a *lektor*, and it would be disingenuous to deny that somewhere murky in my still malleable imagination there was a silent whisper: I was going to be a spy! Let Dr Freud have fun with that.

The Swedish for 'teacher' is *lärare*, and that is what I was. I was a teacher of English as a foreign language to students whom it was still acceptable to describe as housewives and businessmen, in study circles and at night school in a small provincial town in Scandinavia. Was *lärare* an echo of Le Carré? Oh dear.

Was there irony, coincidence or merely a self-fulfilling prophecy in the invitation from the Swedish Royal Navy that came a year later, asking me to narrate a documentary film on a new weapons system? And have I already said too much?

## 22

### lingon *whortleberry*

'lɪn'gɔn

There are debates it is better not to start, arguments you should walk away from. I was too willing for too long to defend 'elk' over 'moose' for the Swedish word *älg* whenever students demanded a definitive answer. I must have wasted hours trying to persuade Swedes that *lagom* can be translated into other languages, and I took too long to stop insisting on 'whortleberry' as a translation for *lingon*. No one I ever met was any the wiser.

So, call it a currant, call it mountain cranberry or insist on whortleberry if it pleases – or why not use the Swedish word and buy a jar of *lingon sylt*, preserve.

As a symbol for the country, its culture and language, the modest lingonberry is a stronger candidate, it seems to me, than the official *Tre Kronor*, Three Crowns, the yellow-and-blue of the national flag, the ubiquitous Dalarna horse or even the elk – sorry, moose – road sign so beloved of Scandinavian fridge magnet manufacturers and sticker makers.

Keep it simple. *Lagom* in all things. A plate of home-made *köttbullar*, Swedish meatballs, or a slice or two of tender braised elk (oh, please!), three or four large boiled potatoes, thick gravy and a very generous spoonful of *lingon*. As the tourist board might say, a taste of Sweden.

It is too many years since I lived in Sweden, and I doubt there has been a single day in all those years when I have not asked myself why I left. I think of my part of the Highlands as Nordic Scotland, and to quote Gavin Maxwell, 'it is no will-o'-the-wisp that I have followed here'. This year, 2021, I have acquired access to a tiny piece of stony scrubland overhung by birch trees and overgrown with clover and Michaelmas daisies and native grasses. My early researches suggest it might offer conditions good enough for *lingon* to thrive. Now to source a handful of plants. A small project emerges. I wonder, will there ever be *lingon* jam for tea in the north-west Scottish Highlands?

## 23

### ljus *candle*

ju:s

My childhood winters were northern, grit-scoured and bitter. Ice, thick ice, often whorled great ferns on the inside of my bedroom window, and the cheap lace curtains, yellow with age and black with mould, sometimes froze onto the glass. These were winters of liberty bodices and chapped legs – no boy under eleven wore long trousers in 1950s Britain. They were winters of cracked lips, chilblains and 'bad chests'. The constant insidious terror of frozen pipes informed our days and bred an obsession with stocks of candles and night lights.

As late as the early 1960s, my great grandmother's house, three streets away from ours, had no electric lighting upstairs, and no hot water supply. In her eighties she still slept under a weight of flannelette sheets, woollen blankets, an eiderdown and a great bedspread, and with a night light burning in a saucer of water placed on the  night stand. The water in the saucer was often frozen solid by dawn.

None of us had bathrooms. All of us had an outside toilet across 'the yard'. On bitter winter nights my mother would place a night light next to the cistern in case it froze overnight, bringing the wrath of the landlord down on us.

And candles were what you kept under the sink in case of power cuts. They came tied with coarse string in thin cardboard boxes from 'the stores' (Co-op) and were as pale and pasty as all our sun-starved complexions.

My first Christmas home from Sweden, I brought candles for everyone. In less than three months of my first Swedish winter I had adopted its candle culture without reservation. Night lights had become tea lights and were dropped inside exquisite crystal 'Snowballs' in comfortable homes and cosy shop windows. Candles here were coloured, shaped and made of thick and creamy stearin. They were functional, yes, but they were also an adornment of these warm, well-furnished, houses and apartments. They were packaged in neat, dark blue boxes with the Swedish royal family's coat-of-arms on them; they were affordable and they were easy to wrap. I had learned how to use *curlingband*, curling ribbon, by watching the quiet shop assistants in Åhléns and NK where gift-wrapping was part of the service. So I gave neatly wrapped small boxes of Liljeholmens *ljus*, candles, to everyone I knew on my return, that Christmas of 1973, that Oil Crisis winter of Edward Heath's three-day week in Britain, of petrol shortages and of power cuts when, I'm sure, my elegant Swedish candles would have been put to good if unexpected use.

## 24

# Lucia
*St Lucy's Day, midwinter celebration of light*

lu'sɪʌ

The twelfth of December 1973 was a Wednesday. The midday temperature was close to minus ten, the luxuriant snow calf-deep. The railbus I had begun to think of as mine – there were so few passengers – had chugged down through the glittering forest from Laxå to arrive at Mariestad's fairy-tale railway station dead on time. It was a short walk up the hill over fat quilts of snow to my wooden house in Kyrkogatan.

I had already learned to leave boots at the bottom of the stairs and my coat by the door before peeling off the layers of jumpers as I trudged up to my rooms. I probably washed yesterday's shirt, fried something, sat by the window to eat it, and started to prepare for my evening class.

I had been in Sweden four months, in Mariestad less than three. I knew almost no one – my landlord's wife and children, my British Centre agent, my students, and, by sight, one or two of the town's shop assistants. I had left a girlfriend and family in England and occasionally I was homesick. But those first winter evenings, when I still wore a university scarf and Aran sweaters and carried my books two or three kilometres through the luminous dark and bitter frosts from one class to the next, belonged only to me. There was no one to require me to share them. I didn't need to explain them or even to analyse them to myself. I would look up at the moon and sometimes wonder whether anyone else I knew, in another city or another country, was looking at it at exactly the same time, but I was hungry for neither company nor events. That whole year in Mariestad had a dreamlike quality about it even at the time, as though I were observing it from outside, from above, not quite grounded in it.

I'd have gone to bed late that night, as usual after teaching. I'd have sat propped up reading Graham Greene, and would eventually have switched off the light and slept.

It couldn't have been earlier than seven the next morning but, woken abruptly from deep sleep by loud, insistent banging on my front door, I was at once disoriented: it felt like three or four o'clock, disarming, alarming, ominous. Knock, knock, knock.

I rolled out of bed, into slippers and fumbled towards the bedroom door in the dark. Stepping onto the landing was like walking into an industrial freezer (I imagine), and I was instantly aware of my naked legs and arms. But the banging on the door was frenzied now, so I winced down the stairs trying not to touch the stair-rail and unable to fully expand my lungs in case they iced up. And still the banging at the door went on, and was that what subtitles would have called indistinct chatter?

There was an outside light above my front door. I pressed the switch as I turned the freezing lock, and opened the door.

It is an overused expression but so apt here: for a moment I really thought I had died in my sleep and was now waking in a kind of Narnia heaven. I didn't count, but in front of me were probably ten, twelve teenage girls, in full-length and to my bleary eyes shimmering white gowns. They were long-haired and blonde and each was softly lit by the flickering candle she was holding. They were ruddy-faced and their winter breath soft-focused them. I must have blinked, maybe shaken my head, maybe rubbed my eyes. And two things suddenly became apparent at once. First, they were all giggling with the cold, seriously shivering but jolly. Second, I *knew* these girls! They were my high school class, and the boys I had only just noticed, some with wizard hats and others dressed in red, were from the same class. Oh, and standing to one side was Lars-Erik, their class teacher, smiling broadly and suddenly ushering everyone into my house and up the stairs. (What was the state of my bedroom? Had I left unwashed cups or worse? What other incriminating detritus of a degenerate life might be there for all to see?)

Still dazed, I followed them upstairs, where a couple of the boys had already poured coffee from an enamel coffee pot and were offering me *lussekater*, saffron buns with raisins, made only at *Lucia*, from under a soft cloth in a birchbark basket. I took the coffee and a bun, but before I could ask even one of the tumble of questions I had, one of the girls, who I now noticed was wearing a crown of (electric) candles and a broad red sash around her waist, began to sing, '*Natten går tunga fjät...*' ('The night walks with a heavy step...'). As the others joined in I was overwhelmed by a sudden compulsion to sob my heart out: the sweet singing in my tiny candlelit room, the pungent coffee, the bitter-tasting saffron buns, the jollity of Lars-Erik whom I didn't really know but who had arranged my first-ever *Lucia* in secret. I thought about how they must at least have liked me enough to do all this for me and I was overwhelmed almost to tears all over again – something that *Lucia* still does to me even now I'm in my seventies.

The thirteenth of December was the shortest day in the old Julian calendar and is still celebrated in Scandinavia as *Lucia*. *Lucia* brings light on the darkest day, a promise of the spring and summer to come.

My students sang their songs, '*Staffan var en stalledräng...*', 'Staffan was a stable-lad...', drank their coffee, ate a plateful of my *pepparkakor*, thin, sweetly spiced biscuits, and were gone in a flurry of snowflakes, almost as though I had imagined it all.

We named our daughter Lucy for *Lucia*, and have celebrated her 'name day' every year since she was born. When she left home for university I took to phoning her each year at seven on the morning of 13 December, and I still do nearly two decades later. When she picks up, I remain silent for the first verse of *Sankta Lucia* which I used to have on cassette and now have on CD and one day I will learn to upload. We talk briefly, hang up and then have a little cry.

## 25

# Mariatorget

*a city park and square in Stockholm*

mʌˈrɪʌˈtɔrjet

Imagine one of those fascinating cut-away drawings from childhood of an old apartment block where you can see into every room: the skinny radiators, the thin ceiling lights, a stove, a kettle boiling, someone taking a steamy bath or shaving in his vest, someone making the bed or reading the morning paper over tea and toast. The janitor is mopping the stairs, a jolly postman makes his way up to the top floor. In the centre of the building there's a caged lift and children playing on every landing, and outside are large-bosomed women walking miniature dogs, butchers and bakers making their deliveries and, in a park with fancy railings and maybe a fountain, young mothers with high prams, someone feeding the pigeons, prim lovers on the grass, a small café and someone on a bike.

Two things come to mind: the delightful illustrations by Ilon Wikland for Astrid Lindgren's 'Bullerby' stories (for the artwork style), and the charming Mariatorget city park and square on Stockholm's south island (for the subject matter).

Mariatorget is, for me, synonymous with *Midnattsloppet*, the Midnight Race, a 10k that I have run a couple of dozen times since the late 1980s. It is held annually on the second Saturday in August. It starts nearby and  passes around the east side of the square before ending just along the road in Hornsgatan. On the night of the race, Mariatorget is evidence that you're going to complete it. It is 'home', it is the crowds and the samba bands, and the public address system, encouraging and informative: 'Bertil Nyqvist is here. This is his fourteenth *Midnattsloppet*. Give him a bit of encouragement to get him over the line. Come on, Bertil!' – that sort of thing.

The following morning, Mariatorget is repossessed by those who live there. It's as though the little square is in denial, pretending that last night's little fling was an aberration – which, actually, it was. Mariatorget normally manages to be both snootily aloof and charmingly down to earth. There's always a small queue at the kiosk for Sunday coffee. The florist does a steady business. The dog-walkers and their high-end pedigree companions are well-dressed and studied in their determination not to look too pleased with themselves. The fountain splatters and the church-goers reward themselves with a pastry from the *konditori* on the corner.

If I could live anywhere in Sweden now, I'd choose a quiet apartment on Mariatorget. One with a tiny balcony, on the sunny side, where I could sit not really reading *Dagens Nyheter*, the Daily News, over strong coffee and a wedge of princess cake, occasionally scribbling a small character sketch in a notebook for my opera, *Mariatorget*, which I will never finish because I enjoy writing it too much to let it end.

## 26

## **motion** *exercise*

mɔt'ʃuːn

They were a pale and lumpen breed, those who brought me up, who inhabited my claustrophobic childhood in The North. Consumptive broken men, arthritic washed-out women old before their time. They talked, through their chain-smoke, of strokes and of thromboses and of other whispered ailments much too grim to say out loud.

No one I knew took exercise. No adult, anyway.

At school we had PT, which halfway through the 1950s became PE. Some of the boys my mother wouldn't let me play with kicked a football around in the parks we called the dene. Some with model parents learned to swim. And later there were cricket teams and rugby teams and sometimes there were sports days when the only thing that mattered was winning, not playing the game. Sport was for competition only. Exercise was suspect.

To move to Sweden, in 1973, was an exercise in forward time travel. In health and welfare they seemed dimensions ahead of us. My students walked to work for exercise. They cycled for good health. At weekends they went orienteering or sailed their modest boats or swam, and in the winter they took to snow and ice like Arctic creatures, skating and skiing for the exhilaration of being in motion. *Motion*, therefore, seems so appropriate a word for exercise in Swedish, emphasising movement over competition or dubious notions of esprit de corps.

Everywhere I have lived in Sweden there have been illuminated communal running tracks that double as cross-country ski courses in the winter. There have been ice-rinks, forest walks, lakeside paths, cycle routes and tennis courts, and I could write at length about the place of *motion* in Swedish culture and society. But I can't resist the story of G, one of my early students in Mariestad.

Social invitations were sometimes little more than thinly disguised bids for free English lessons. If we met for coffee outside of class, no one ever insisted we communicate solely in Swedish (it would have been a strained encounter). G was keen. He had limited but aspirational English. He was also a proficient cross-country skier and believed it would be good for me to learn. One evening after class, G held back while the other students left. It was poor etiquette to invite the teacher out in front of fellow students. So G waited and then came forward with his carefully rehearsed invitation: 'Stephen, I would be very pleased if you would like to do a motion with me on the forest track on Saturday.' There are times when, even as a language teacher, you don't quite have the heart to correct.

## 27

# musik *music*
mu'si:k


In the 1970s, being a native speaker and knowing four guitar chords was qualification enough for a language teaching post in the private sector pretty much anywhere. At the end of my first-ever Swedish lesson in Stockholm, Mats, the slim young teacher in a cheesecloth shirt, brought out his guitar and I braced myself for a blast of Nordic *Kumbaya*.

Instead, I heard and immediately learned the first example of what was to become my moderate repertoire of Swedish music, *Vem kan segla?* [Traditional]. My translation: 'Who can Sail?'

> Vem kan segla förutan vind?
>> *Who can sail without the wind?*
> Vem kan ro utan åror?
>> *Who can row without oars?*
> Vem kan skiljas från vännen sin
>> *Who can leave a friend behind*
> Utan att fälla tåror?
>> *Without the shedding of tears?*

Jag kan segla förutan vind;

> *I can sail without the wind;*

Jag kan ro utan åror,

> *I can row without oars*

Men ej skiljas från vännen min

> *But I can't leave a friend behind*

Utan att fälla tåror.

> *Without the shedding of tears.*

A couple of years on, another end-of-course present-for-the-teacher was an LP, *Bergtagen*, bewitched, spirited away into the magic mountain, by Merit Hemmingson and her band Folkmusikgruppen – a kind of Swedish Steeleye Span meets Fairport Convention. One of my students was a graphic designer and she'd made a replica of the record, grooves and all, in cardboard, as a gift card to accompany the present, with the students' names 'credited' on the record label – all hand-drawn and cut, and decorated with folk motifs from Dalarna, coloured with marker pens. On my first visit back to the UK, I guested on a chat show on BBC Radio Tees to talk a bit about living and working in Sweden, and I played a track from the album, *Jämtländsk Brudmarsch '73*, 'Wedding March from Jämtland, '73', still a favourite, along with everything by Jan Johansson and, much more recently, the Swedish-Norwegian a capella group Trio Mediæval. If you Google nothing else from this page, do check out *Du är den första*, 'You Are the First', by Arve Henriksen and Trio Mediæval.

I sat alone in the back office of Motell Hasslerör, halfway between Mariestad and Hova, on the evening of Saturday 6 April 1974, watching TV while my friend, the motel manager and self-styled 'Old C(r)ook' was smashing out the Elephant Ears in the kitchen. Erik had been a cook in the Swedish merchant navy and might have been the original model for the expression 'rough diamond'. Elephant Ears were his signature dish. Steaks, salted to near-transparency and then mercilessly beaten so flat and thin that there could have been little left but meat fibre. They were flash-fried and served with boiled potatoes, thick gravy and a large dollop of *lingon sylt*. Erik, the old sea-dog, was – inexplicably – married to M, one of the most glamorous Swedish women I ever met. A Nigella Lawson lookalike. M had lived in England and had bred borzois or salukis or Afghan hounds or all three for the 1960s model Jean Shrimpton.

Erik was an awkward man who had a troubled relationship with alcohol, but he was exceptionally generous to both me and my disabled mother (in the UK) whom he never met.

So I was often to be found of a Saturday evening sitting in that back office, watching the little black-and-white portable TV placed there among invoices for 'chicken dogs' and *Falukorv*, while Erik worked.

But this was no ordinary Saturday night. This was the night that ABBA won the Eurovision Song Contest, across the North Sea and down a bit, in Brighton. The world changed that evening. Not right away perhaps: I rang my mother on Erik's office phone, for which I'm sure either Shell or ICA paid the bill, and she was characteristically unimpressed. Me too, to be honest.

Forty years on, however, I still thrill every time the Arlanda Express pulls out of Stockholm Airport on its twenty-minute dash to Central Station and we are all welcomed onboard by the urbane voice of sweet Björn Ulvaeus. Instant nostalgia and, for me at least, the perfect welcome back to my spiritual home.

# 28

## när öppet *convenience store*
'næ:r'əpet

All the world loves a *kanelbulle,* a Swedish cinnamon bun, it seems. Friends of mine bake their own, and make a decent job of it. There are recipes in every book of Swedish food, and you can pick them up in British coffee shops and cafés now, as though they have always been here. They have not.

They surfed in on the crest of the flat-pack furniture wave, just behind the *köttbullar,* meatballs, the *senapssill,* herring in mustard sauce, and those *pepparkakor,* ginger biscuits no one really likes. But in every Swedish school I ever worked in there was a staffroom coffee table under a low light in the corner, and on that table there was always a basket of fresh *kanelbullar* next to the *servietter,* paper napkins, and the box of *sockerbitar,* rock-hard sugar cubes, that don't dissolve in any liquid safe to drink. I ate them – the *kanelbullar* – and drank the laxative coffee, and worked off the rest of the calories trying to teach reluctant teenagers and dashing across Stockholm from school to school. I was young.

When I moved into my girlfriend's penthouse apartment in a swanky part of town, I found there was a *när öppet,* convenience store, on the ground floor, and what was convenient about it was that apart from being open (the *öppet* bit) through the night, it also sold cinnamon buns.

These were not just regular, bakery-and-coffee-shop cinnamon buns, these were mini-buns in family packs. And if the fresh-baked confections of the school staffrooms were moreish, these were of an altogether higher order of addiction.

Imagine you've a fresh pack of Plasticine and you take out the yellow strip and the brown strip. You soften them up a bit and then roll them like a Swiss roll, with the brown strip on the inside. Cut the roll in half and you have a mini *kanelbulle* lookalike. Damp to the touch and slightly tacky, it even feels like a Pågens miniature cinnamon bun.

I haven't made them sound appetising, but it was not unusual for one of us to slip on clothes and take the lift down to the ground floor at three in the morning to pop into the 'when open' for a bag – or more. Some of our friends smoked dope; we got high on cinnamon buns. I blame the *när öppet*, of course. Nothing to do with the intemperance of youth.

Which doesn't help explain how if you put a bag of them in front of me right now, I'd polish off the lot before the evening's done.

## 29

**osthyvel** *cheese slice*

'ʊst'hyvel

I have let it be known that I want my ashes scattered in Mariatorget, the charming bourgeois garden-square on *Södermalm*, Stockholm's south island, but I already left a little bit of myself in Sweden one evening in 1993, when I sliced the top off my thumb with a brand new *osthyvel*, cheese slice, and watched it disappear down the kitchen sink in a small town in Dalarna. Thirty years on, I still have no sensation in the tip of my left thumb.

A strong form of the Sapir-Whorf hypothesis – a favourite with students of linguistics – might be said to speculate on the degree to which an object is perceptible if we don't have a word for it. My old English master, Joe Bateman, put a sixpence on his teacher's desk one day in 1964 and tried to persuade us that if we didn't know the words 'sixpence', 'coin' and 'money', we wouldn't have noticed the sixpence there on the desk.

Unlike Benjamin Lee Whorf's, my (unconscious) researches were carried out not among the North American Hopi but between the aisles of the ICA, EPA and Konsum supermarkets that framed the town square in Mariestad.

In the same way that I literally overlooked cans of *surströmming*, sour fermented herring, and boxes of *snus*, a smokeless tobacco product placed in the mouth, because I had no vocabulary with which to identify or describe them, so with the *osthyvel*, until I saw one in use in a friend's kitchen. On returning to my own kitchen, I immediately spotted what must have been there since I moved in, among the corkscrews and whisks and pastry brushes in the cutlery drawer: an *osthyvel*. I went through two blocks of cheese at once, then graduated to cucumbers and carrots and, with somewhat less success, bananas.

To compensate for the cheese slice having been invented by a Norwegian, Thomas Bjørklund, in 1925, Swedes like to tell of his Norwegian meanness with the cheese rather than his carpenter's obsession with cutting a slice of consistent thickness. Whatever his motivation, Thomas Bjørklund gave Sweden one of its best-recognised symbols of national identity – and its sharpest.

# __30

## **pimpling** *ice fishing (sort of)*
'pɪmplɪŋ

Words mean what a language community agrees they mean. Dictionary definitions are a manifestation of such agreement. In *Through the Looking-Glass*, Lewis Carroll gives Humpty Dumpty a provocative line of dialogue:

'When *I* use a word,' Humpty Dumpty said, in a rather scornful tone, 'it means just what I choose it to mean – neither more nor less.'

I am not a fisherman and I have probably never been required to talk about the sport, if that is quite the right word (ask Humpty Dumpty). But during that first winter in Sweden, when Lake Vänern froze solid and I drove a car on the ice for the first time, I also saw my first ice-fisher. Like some nodding toy you might spot on the dashboard of a passing timber truck, it was a fur-hooded figure bent over a neat hole in the ice and drooping a line down into the water way below. Lying beside him (I'm assuming it was a man) on the ice was a giant drill bit, a couple of metres long and shiny as a new blue tractor.

My companion, a student whose Peugeot 404 I'd just been spinning across the ice the way you'd drive the dodgems at a fairground, told me this was *pimpling*, and, of course, I smirked.

*Pimpling*, a word I'd never need but was never going to forget. *Pimpling*, so inappropriate a word for such a hardy endeavour as fishing through a hole in ice a metre thick at minus fifteen Celsius (I suppose you know that Celsius was a Swede). *Pimpling*, a word more suited to mime or dance manoeuvres or a way of gently mocking. *Pimpling*, a word you'll not forget now, either.

Over the years, I have dropped *pimpling* into conversations where trivia or light relief were required, and in the interests of accuracy I have just taken down my Swedish dictionary to check. And I am horrified to find that ice fishing translates not as *pimpling* at all but as *isfiske* – as you might expect: *is* = ice and *fiske* = fish. My first thought now was that I have been the victim all these years of a well-intentioned joke at my expense. And I quite like that.

In the dictionary, *pimpling* referred me to *pimpelfiske* and that is defined as 'jigging'. Perhaps my suggestion of a dance manoeuvre wasn't so far off the mark. To return to the looking-glass:

'The question is,' said Alice, 'whether you *can* make words mean so many different things.'

It turns out that *pimpling* is ice fishing with a very particular kind of lure, one you have to 'jig' with the wrist. So not a practical joke then, after all. A bit of me is rather disappointed.

Humpty Dumpty was almost certainly a monoglot with limited life experience. Alice, as always, got closer to a truth. If my fifty words for love in Swedish demonstrate anything at all, it is that words carry with them rather more than dictionary definitions. They carry, in our careful choice of them, the times and places and people we have known. They echo familiar voices and sentimental music; they carry on the air the scent of newly fallen snow; of pickled herring or strong coffee; of cinnamon buns or dill. They taste of books and foreign postage stamps and grit. They make us cry. They make us laugh. And words like *pimpling* never fail to lift the spirits.

Stephen Keeler

# Part 4

The end of the academic year comes early in Sweden. It is timed to coincide with *Midsommar*, the most important public holiday of the year, around the third weekend in June. Even in southern Sweden it is not often really quite warm enough for the *Midsommar* celebrations of dancing and fiddle music and, weather-permitting, eating and drinking out of doors. But Swedes are hardy folk: I have seen maypole dancing in snow as far south as Dalarna at *Midsommar*. I have also celebrated *Midsommar* bathed in the yellow sunlight of the Swedish flag, under the blue of its skies, warmed as though by the benign breath of the Nordic gods themselves, and as charming as a picture-book childhood.

At the end of my first, and as it turned out only, year in Mariestad, the afternoon ladies decided we would have a picnic instead of a final lesson. I was instructed to do nothing, to bring nothing and to prepare no lesson. I would be picked up in one of the ageing but spotless Mercedes and we would drive out into the countryside near Kinnekulle, the only hill in Västergötland (though local folk like, mockingly, to call it a mountain), half an hour or so by car from Mariestad.

My memories of that day are patchy but filled with remembered warmth. The fertile farmlands of Västergötland are not so different from the North Yorkshire-South Durham countryside of my childhood: a little flatter, perhaps, a little wider, with bigger skies, but not alien. It was a bright day, hot in the sun but still icy out of it. My ladies knew where they were going and where to park, and were business-like and efficient in unpacking the baskets and boxes, the bottles and blankets, and in no time at all a splendid picnic was set out before me like something from a movie of 'that summer'. There was a box of chicken portions, chilled, individually wrapped in squares of foil and loosely swaddled in a linen cloth. There were small quiches with cream cheese and anchovy and stuffed olives. There was a huge wedge of *Herrgårds Ost* cheese, a small slab of *smör*, hand-patted butter, *knäckebröd*, crispbread, and a loaf of home-baked crusty bread. There were slender strips of neatly trimmed celery, and small, sweet tomatoes and crisp lettuce and more cheese and small cuts of herring in dill-mustard cream sauce. There were crinkle-cut slivers of sweet cucumber, and there was a little tub of bright pink beetroot salad, a handful of hard-boiled egg halves and a tube of Kalles Kaviar. I have made it sound lavish, and in a sense it was, and exotic to the idiot boy from a northern town who looked on in gormless bewilderment, determined not to betray his ignorance.

But there was nothing in excess. There were twelve of us and there were twelve of everything: twelve small chicken pieces, twelve palm-sized quiches, twelve portions of salad ... and twelve wooden butter knives for scouring out a whorl of butter and handing it to your neighbour – a custom I immediately found delightful and have practised ever since. There were twelve soft cotton napkins, twelve picnic glasses and twelve bottles of thoughtfully selected soft drinks. It had been assumed that I would drink a Three Towns *mellanöl* – a low-alcohol and zero-flavour beer that was ubiquitous in Sweden in those days – since I wasn't driving. But the ladies all had fruit sodas or Ramlösa mineral water, before the Thermos flasks were brought out and boiled coffee was poured for each, without asking, and sweet buns sprinkled with *pärl socker*, pearl sugar, were passed around in a basket of woven birchbark lined with a thin towel. There was even a small box of *bit socker*, sugar lumps of a kind I have only ever come across in Scandinavia, which don't appear to dissolve no matter how hot the coffee or how long you leave them. Everything was just right. *Lagom*, in fact.

We sat on the thick blankets in the sun and I ate their lovely food and drank their awful beer and kept reminding myself that this was my job. They had even bought me a small present, wrapped in the yellow and blue wrapping paper of the porcelain and crystal shop in town and tied with the first curling ribbon I had ever seen. It was a lead crystal 'Snowball' candle-holder, the first of what was to become, over the next twenty years, a large and prized collection. And then we went for a short walk across the open meadow towards the small forest.

Where I come from, 'dandelion' meant one thing, bed-wetting. You picked a dandelion, you'd wet the bed. Simple, uncomplicated, unsophisticated, a bit brutal. Like so much of childhood.

Naturally, enough, this mythology coloured my perception of the flower. I should say here that, in common with many primary schoolchildren of 1950s Britain, I knew a lot about wildflowers, and I still do. We'd had enlightened teachers who took us out of school to pick flowers in spring for pressing, and leaves in the autumn for drying. These were the salad days of Ladybird Books, and I-Spy, and, later, the Observer's Books of everything 'natural'. Our parents and grandparents would have thought it an unexceptional skill to be able to name any wildflower they came across, and I grew up knowing primroses and wood anemones and coltsfoot just as I knew the names of the streets where I lived and played.

A Swedish spring is stippled with wildflowers. There are still wildflower meadows and hedgerows and large areas of countryside not much troubled by destructive human activity, and there are protected areas and protected species, and on Kinnekulle there were wild orchids that were so rare their positions were mapped and tiny wooden fences made out of what looked to me like lollipop sticks erected around them when they came up in the spring. This is what the ladies took me to see on our little walk after the picnic, and on the way across the meadow they pointed out other wild-flowers and I gave them their names in English while they told me what each was called in Swedish. That afternoon I learned *vitsippa*, wood anemone, *blåsippa*, hepatica, *påsk lilja*, daffodil (literally Easter lily), *jord viva*, primrose, and *mask ros*, dandelion, and for no convincing reason I can think of, it was *mask ros* that I not only remembered but that became the token of remembrance, the signifier for the whole of that raw but fertile year in Mariestad. The memento of an enduring love affair with an entire country.

# ___ 31

**porslin** *porcelain, crockery, tableware, china*
pɔʃˈliːn

The objects that detain us awhile, that find their way to us if you believe in Fate, acquire a language they share with us for as long as the relationship lasts.

Yvonne gave me a splendid Russian St Nicholas 'doll' made of clay, exquisitely painted and glazed and with a small clapper on a thread inside that rings like a tinker-bell when the doll is shaken. It was the last Christmas present she would buy me, and it speaks to me, whenever I care to listen, in the language of things, perched up there on top of my bookshelf. Like the eider duck we bought in Malmö forty-odd years ago.

The eider duck is the loveliest object I own, and I frequently take it from the hall table just to cradle it in both hands. Designed by Paul Hoff (1945- ) and made by the venerable Gustavsberg ceramics company, it is what the Swedes call *porslin*. For once, I don't care whether it is 'china' or 'porcelain' or 'pottery' or 'ceramic': it is simply beautiful to look at and settling to hold.

And like so many of my words of love in Swedish, *porslin* is one I like to make with my mouth and voice. It has the quality of slip, of glaze, of shiny pottery – *porslin*.

After decades of wanting to own a companion piece –
the handsomest grebe, also by Paul Hoff – but failing
for all those years to pay attention to its persistent
voice, I have just today bought it for my friend's new
house. An interesting way of putting it, as though I am
giving it to the house that will almost certainly outlive
the friend.

My daughter will inherit my Gustavsberg eider. The
language it speaks will remain accessible a little longer.
I am occasionally overwhelmed with sadness – a kind
of mourning – for objects, even cheap souvenirs,
that are orphaned or widowed. It is a loss that robs
them of the power of speech, the way memories are
condemned to haunt the void forever once the last one
to know them has died.

I pick up my *porslin* eider. I hold it firmly in both hands,
its face pointing forward, as though I were making an
offering of it.

## 32

**puss och kram** *kiss and hug*

'pus ɔ 'krɑːm

The love letter is a thing of the past. Museums will
be built to it, in time. It is a disappearing genre, as
faded as the blue-black ink we wrote in, as quaint and
inconvenient as the fountain pens we cherished when
to write a letter in ballpoint ink still brought with it a
whiff of shame.

I wrote my weekly letter home on lined *Tre Kronor*,
Three Crowns, paper. The envelopes were deckle-edged
and lined with fine grey tissue, and nothing I had to say
could ever do it justice.

Letters took a week to get to Britain, replies another
week to get to me. The life in anything I'd written a
fortnight ago would have expired long before I got a
letter in reply. And so a lukewarm love affair with J, the
girlfriend I had left behind in England, evaporated in
the mail somewhere over the North Sea.

It was some time before I found myself looking forward
to the post again. But K was a romantic with loopy
Swedish handwriting and a deftness with a gel pen
and a coloured heart – precursor to the emoji, I guess.
The first letter I opened from her, in English that was
pretty hit-and-miss but I could let that go for now,
ended, alarmingly, *puss och kram*, and I'm pretty sure

I blushed before reaching for the dictionary. *Puss*, thank god, meant 'kiss', and *kram* seemed appropriate enough for 'hug': cram?

It was the first of a small batch of letters that stopped abruptly when it was clear that I was moving on. She found herself a fork-lift truck driver at the Electrolux factory whose prospects seemed hugely better than mine.

## 33

# pytt i panna *hash*

ˈpyt ɪ ˈpʌnʌ

*Pytt i panna*, hash, just for the name of it, for the frisson of pronouncing its fairy-tale sounds. *Pytt i panna*, literally small bits in a pan, was a standard on the menu at Motell Hasslerör, which stood on the motorway that grazed the outskirts of Mariestad, and where my student Erik, married to the glamorous M, was the manager.

Erik, whom we've already met, was never a chef, but in his kitchen there was something choreographic about this giant of a man, permanently stooped from his years commanding cramped galleys on board merchant navy ships, and with hands the size and shape and colour of boiled hams. When Erik came into a room it became a doll's house. Towering above his hotplate, a careless spatula in one hand and a wizened roll-up in the other, Erik lumbered about his kitchen, never making an unnecessary move. Scraping, flicking, shovelling the bits of stuff he fried – and frying was his favourite medium – he'd produce a plate of *pytt i panna* looking like a textbook illustration in the time it took his waitresses to scribble down the next order.

Topped with a couple of slices of crinkled beetroot and a sunny-side-up egg, the fried pork and potato 'leftovers' had truck-driver appeal, and, satisfied with his art, Erik would stand back, take a long and wincing drag on his roll-up and disappear into his office for half a tumbler of cheap Bulgarian red and a flash of his perpetual daydream of a rolling, roving life at sea.

Erik wore his melancholy the way a fallen angel wears a tarnished halo. You saw it in his eyes: childlike and gentle and lost on land, as though forever looking for the favourite toy that had been snatched from him while he was looking the other way.

## 34

**raggare** *hot-rod driver, greaser, rocker*

'rʌgʌre

In the land of *lagom*, the *raggare*, hot-rod driver, phenomenon was both unlikely and unsurprising.

Like many boys who grew up in 1950s Britain, I had an extensive collection of Dinky and Corgi die-cast model cars. Each model had its unique character, and most were North American – the blowsy Plymouth taxi cab with whitewall tyres, the street-smart Studebaker Golden Hawk, the lumbering Buick. I learned to read from their little boxes – Made in England; Patent Pending – and from the legends printed on some of them – Heinz 57 Varieties; Express Dairies. I loved them all. They were all I had, apart from coloured pencils and broken board games. I can still feel the ridges of their roofs between the tip of the index finger and thumb of my right hand as I propelled them gently across the chenille tablecloth in my great-granny's front room. And like a bad parent, I had a favourite: the 1959 Chevrolet Impala Highway Patrol car, done out in black and white police livery and with a plastic aerial on the back wing.

We had been the first in our street to get TV – my father was a salesman – and I had watched Broderick Crawford as Dan Mathews in *Highway Patrol*. Now I could act out its plotless dramas in stop-action detail on the front room table, and it was formative stuff.

My first-ever evening in Stockholm, the rain had stopped and the late sun briefly gilded the rooftops. I was drawn outdoors by the charm of it, and set off for a stroll towards the centre of town. The boulevard trees along Sveavägen were freshly laundered, and sodium street lights seemed to lend romance to every shadow. The high-stacked plate-glass windows of the new downtown office blocks of Hötorget and Sergels Torg glittered with futuristic promise, but at street level I became aware of a deep-throated rumbling and sudden blasts of rock 'n' roll. I turned the corner into Kungsgatan, and it was as though I had wandered onto the set of *Rebel Without A Cause*.

Mirrored neon cinema facades caught the yellow street light and reflected it onto the stretched bonnets of a dozen or more sleek and growling 1950s US cars, the cars from my granny's front room table. There were Buicks and a Lincoln Continental, a Cadillac Fleetwood and a marvellous Pontiac. There were Bel-Airs and Mustangs and an Edsel, and within touching distance there was my first-ever in-the-flesh 1959 Chevrolet Impala.

It was cherry red and shiny as lip gloss and the girl in black leather in the passenger seat had her feet out of the window and the most studied pout you could imagine. I was still a kid from County Durham: it took me a while to take this in.

What I had come across was the Friday night square-mile cruise of the *raggare* – a word difficult to translate satisfactorily, not least because this was a purely Scandinavian phenomenon and one that has passed, like the Mods and the Rockers of Brighton beach.

*Raggare* were variously described to me by those in my respectable ladies' study circles as 'hooligans', 'Teddy Boys', 'degenerates' and 'young layabouts', and for a while the *raggare* phenomenon was cause for real enough concern in Stockholm and small-town Sweden. Like the police procedural novels of Per Wahlöö and Maj Sjöwall I had yet to discover, the *raggare* were an emblem of dissent in a country of perceived drab and dangerous conformity. I marvelled at the ra-ra skirts and black leather of the girlfriends, the fishnet tights and occasional rhinestones, and was impressed by the overt consumption of beer – albeit practically alcohol-free beer – in a country where public displays of most kinds were not quite done. I envied the drivers (almost always men) their fine cars, and recognised with respect the hours they must have spent on raising suspensions, restoring bodywork, fine-tuning engines – no layabouts, these. I have never seen so much denim in one place.

Where are they now, these young tearaways and their flighty molls? Like the rest of us, they grew older and some a little more respectable. A few will have married and most of them will have got somewhere of their own to live and raise a family, but if you happen to be in Rättvik at the end of July for its Classic Car Week you'll find them. Not as skinny as they were, or as shiny, and the thick, greased hair may have thinned and paled. The girlfriends now might bring along their grandchildren, but the cars are still the same. Better, for they are cherished like pedigree livestock.

# 35

## rea *sale*

reʌ

It was a little word for joy back in those not-quite-carefree days of penniless youth. *Rea*, slapped across shop windows at dramatic angles, like the POW! in a Batman comic, suggested that outrageous bargains might be had inside. The harsh reality was that even in a sale nothing much was cheap in Sweden, and anything we ever wanted was never included in the sale anyway.

The exception, the *rea* that characterised my Stockholm years, were the *bok rea*.

Hedengrens Bokhandel bookshop was and remains my smart Stockholm bookshop of choice. Its modest-prosperous frontage, at Stureplan in the upmarket Östermalm district, has the old school gravitas of a university library. Its window displays of the latest fiction and coffee-table books of Swedish landscape are irresistible. Its downstairs cave of hushed delights is therapeutic. The lighting is subdued. They play no music. Even boisterous children quieten under its muted colours and its sound-absorbing walls.

I go to Hedengrens for European fiction and illustrated children's books in Swedish, but there are leather-backed journals and fountain pens you wouldn't buy just to write with; there are academic diaries and wallcharts numbering the weeks, as Sweden does. It is a place to go before you go for coffee. Go alone. Spend. Don't visit Hedengrens for the *rea*.

There were, though, entire book chains whose business model was to move large quantities of often large books at discount prices. There was one such discount emporium in Odengatan, round the corner from our Birger Jarlsgatan apartment. It specialised in art books and the movies, and in the couple of years we lived there we amassed a stack of the Hollywood greats, biographies of moon-faced matinée idols and the silent goddesses of the silver screen. I learned about film noir, the musicals of MGM and everything that Bogart had appeared in. We bought scripts and glossy volumes of the fan photos the studios sent out; histories of cinema and the architecture of the dream palaces; and documentary texts from which I learned that a man like me could move to California to be a chauffeur to the stars and drive around all day dressed in jodhpurs in a Cadillac Fleetwood in the sun...

For five *kronor* you could pick up a coffee-table book bigger than our coffee table on Matisse, Monet, Toulouse-Lautrec. And we did. We had art and we had movies and we bought travel books on Sweden. It was our accidental second degree course, without the angst of final exams. When it was time to go, we left them all behind, our bargain basement books. They'd served their purpose, but I miss them and never fail to pause at the plate-glass windows when I'm in Stockholm and there's a *bok rea*. It's like lingering at the Dinky Toys, the Meccano and the Bayko in a museum of childhood and wanting to stop everyone there and tell them, 'I used to have this when I was a kid.'

## 36

___

**Saab** *a brand of car*

saːb

If I were a writer of detective fiction, my down-at-heel sleuth would own a Saab. She might have a doctorate in entomology, a cottage inherited from a distant relative on an abandoned island in the Stockholm archipelago, and the suggestion of a failed attempt at religion – you can see why I'm not a writer of detective fiction – and she'd also have a Saab 96. The adjectives 'battered' and 'colourless' would have to accompany any description of it, and it would frequently have to be off the road for repair. Which is unfair and inaccurate because if ever a car was designed to function in extreme weather conditions and simply keep on going, it is a Saab. Look how often it won the RAC and Monte Carlo rallies in the 1960s.

Social democratic Sweden made much of its classlessness, and while it is certainly true that many of the inbuilt inequalities of industrial societies were systematically reduced if not entirely eradicated in mid-twentieth-century Sweden, subtle indicators always float to the surface.

The elderly ladies of my afternoon classes in Mariestad and Stockholm were leisured, and owned those not-quite-new Mercedes (as we know, a new one would have been crass and simply unnecessary). Those with

Bohemian pretensions drove a Saab. Only those who had to work for a living drove a Volvo. No one took you seriously if you owned a foreign car.

One of my earliest students owned an ancient British Leyland Mini – the Swedes called them a *hundkoja*, dog kennel. Poor Lars. As if his walrus moustache, his appalling nylon clothes and his not quite faint enough body odour weren't enough, he owned a Mini! He was a pilot. Had access to a small plane. He was young and well paid. The moustache notwithstanding, he wasn't bad looking. He could fix most things and could even play the fiddle. But he had a foreign car. Worse, he had a British car, at a time when they'd become synonymous with unreliability and poor build-quality. A British Mini. Way beyond the pale.

# 37

## **sambo** *live-in partner*

'sʌmbʊ

I met Yvonne, the woman who would later agree to marry me, in an upper room above a cake shop in Stockholm. She had the worst David Bowie haircut I had ever seen, and on the hottest day of that city summer she was wearing a thick black skirt that touched the ground.

It was 1974 and I had not yet learned not to wear nylon shirts, half-unbuttoned. Her long skirt was to conceal the thousand inflamed mosquito bites she'd got at a country picnic the day before. The stuff that love is made of.

By the following summer I had moved into Yvonne's smart penthouse apartment. We had become each other's *sambo*, live-in partner, a functional word for love in Swedish, clumsily welded together from two bits of two other words: *sam-* from *samman*, together, and *-bo*, from *boende*, living accommodation. An early poem of mine reanimates our first *sambo* Christmas:

## Sleeping Together

*Stockholm 1975*

That year we lugged a fine sprung tree across
the dashing evening city, resting now
and then in quilted snow on cushioned walls
around the National Library by the park
and covered-market steps.

She leaned against a street lamp fumbling for
an extra pair of gloves and I held on
the tree becoming whiter as I stood
and watched the lumbering buses on their way
to suburbs such as ours.

At some unspoken signal of assent
still new to us and bright with strange comfort
we shook the tree and slung it once again
between us like a now-becoming pair
of practised foresters.

She coaxed the tree indoors and knew at once
to hold the glossy crown as though it were
a newborn infant's head. We propped it on
the frosted balcony where in summer
we'd first sunbathed naked.

We slept that night drugged with trust and
  careless
with the door ajar and woke to find a
snow dune draped across the corner of the
room and up against the wardrobe door like
a shrouded drunk asleep.

Like six-year-olds on Christmas Eve we whooped
and scooped up snow from carpet and
  floorboards
and flung it like the fizz in sparkling wine.
I lobbed a gentle indoor snowball like
a taboo shattering.

# ___38

## semla *Lenten bun*

'semlʌ

It is February. I am writing this more than usually cut off from the outside world, on the far north-west coast of Scotland. Overnight, drifts have blocked the only road. The snow gates are closed at Braemore Junction and, as far as I know, I am at least 500 miles from the nearest *semla*. The clock is ticking. I have about a month.

Here, there were hot cross buns on sale in August, and that is unequivocally wrong. I won't have tulips in the house before New Year nor egg-shaped chocolate after Easter. And in Sweden I found a like-minded culture. In her recipe for Swedish Lenten buns, my friend Brontë Aurell writes: 'You will never ever find *semlor* sold outside the season – it is just not done.' And she is right.

It was one more endearing aspect of Swedish culture: no Christmas stuff before Advent, no *kräftor*, crayfish, except in August, and no *semlor* outside Lent. I loved how spring gathered towards *Midsommar* the way plants grow towards the light, how towns and cities emptied in July as families decamped to their *sommarstugor*, summer cottages, and how you joined a self-improving evening course every September. The Swedish calendar became comforting in its predictability.

I ate my first *semla* in Laxå. I barely knew what Lent was, having been brought up in a Methodist household where such things were dismissed as 'high church'. Pancake Tuesday was a Tuesday in March when we had three days off school and on one of them – I never questioned it – my mother made pancakes, gritted them with sugar and doused them in 'juice' from a plastic lemon which I fidgeted to use later as a water pistol.

It was my first Swedish spring, and I arrived at Börje Stern's house in Laxå as usual one Wednesday in February for early dinner before teaching my evening class. Börje was the British Centre's representative in Laxå. He recruited my students, booked the classrooms and arranged overnight accommodation for me in a pleasant *pension* (B&B). He was also a high school teacher of English and German, and a writer of very successful language teaching textbooks.

I had seen *semlor* (plural of *semla*) packed onto trays in the window of the *bageri*, bakery, in the street where I lived in Mariestad. Suggesting the bulging rosy cheeks of plump country girls, they were powdered with icing sugar and luxuriant as stuffed pillows after spring cleaning. But I had no idea that the bread was bittersweet with a hint of cardamom, nor that under that fat cap of thick, piped fresh whipped cream was a soft and melting heart of marzipan.

I just had to stop writing for a moment to compose myself...

*Semlor* purists have told me that my first experience was how they should be eaten – Börje's silent wife served mine, like a small devotion, in a soup bowl with a spoon, and poured a cupful of warm milk around it. I still quite like my *semlor* served that way, but very little in life, I have found, beats taking your strong black coffee and your tea plate with a *semla* and cake fork on it to your discreet table in the corner of the *konditori* and, well, just diving straight in.

If the snow melts and I can make the trip to London before Easter, my first stop – quite possibly before I offload my luggage – will be to any one (or all) of the half-dozen Swedish bakeries I know where there are cardamom-infused, marzipan-filled, cream-topped buns with my name on them.

## 39

# Skattungbyn
*a dot on the map in rural Dalarna*
'skʌtuŋ'byn

I do hope I am not imagining this, the way some apparent episodes in one's life remain convincing half a century after they were first dreamed.

There is a dot on the map a couple of dozen kilometres along the road from Furudal to Orsa, in Dalarna, central Sweden, with the name Skattungbyn. In my memory of images it is little more than a road sign, a lay-by with a view, and a roadside café closed down a generation ago.

I drove that road on Friday afternoons over a twenty-year period when I worked for Lennart Öhnell at his unique Garden-of-Eden centre of enlightened education, Furudals Bruks Kursinternat. The drive through the glittering pine forest to Orsa, for a cup of coffee and a wedge of *Prinsesstårta*, was a necessary indulgence after a week of claustrophobically intensive language 'training' with high-status and sometimes very demanding students.

Lennart never refused me the car. Alone among the repertory company of language-teaching specialists who worked for him, I hated 'The Spectacular' – the name we gave to his ageing, brick-like Fiat 132, hand-painted all over with rustic images of *Midsommar* dancers in traditional costume, and forever infused with the pungent aromas of Lennart's Irish wolfhound, Jenny who lived in the car the rest of the time. So it would be his proletarian Toyota, or the madness on skinny wheels that was his venerable Citröen, which would crunch the gravel in the small off-road car park of the shop I began to call the 'museum shop' at Skattungbyn, on the rare occasions it was open when I passed that way.

I have no idea of its history, who owned it or how its stock was acquired. It appeared to have a season that coincided with the short northern summer, and having been a grey pencil sketch since September it became a delightful watercolour from late May. There were cornflowers and nasturtiums growing wild around the wooden step, and more nasturtiums tumbling from fat glazed pots out front. There were early Michaelmas daisies and some wild strawberries too, but it is easy to drift into a Lena Anderson *Linnea* illustration so we will step inside...

... to a time before television and motorised transport, when diversion was frivolous and needs had to be met. I don't know whether the dozens of pairs of elemental ice-skates hanging from hooks in the roof timbers were for sale. Nor the skis or snow shoes or wooden rakes and long-handled shovels which might never have been new but were here, scrubbed as though for Sunday church, and stacked in military-precise ranks along the back wall where drawer-fronts announced their contents – nails and screws and wire; doorknobs and handles, bolts and hinges and locks; spinning-tops and marbles. And then the roll call of Sweden's industrial heritage announced in enamel advertisements nailed to the walls, for Crescent, Monark and Kronan  bicycles, for Stiga lawnmowers and, later, table-tennis kit; Husqvarna, Electrolux, Ericsson. But by now someone had appeared at the massive counter, behind the Facit cash register, and my attention was drawn to the stuff I knew to be for sale, the home-made cakes, the raspberry cordial and the hand-knitted dolls.

I may have imagined the *badhus*, bathhouse, road sign, and I may have romanced into existence the battered Volvo, colourless in the blizzard, heading home with a huge Christmas tree tied to the roof and a bundle of jolly, red-faced children inside, but I did not imagine the museum shop at Skattungbyn, for I have in my hand one of the half-dozen knitted dolls I bought for Lucy in the summers I was there alone, or that we bought together when she was with us in her Maja yellow oilskin and painted *träskor*, wooden clogs, from Nils Olsson in Mora.

What seemed so charming then is almost grotesque now. The blancmange-pink face, red-slash mouth and bulbous nose might have been modelled on some old woman's husband, I suppose. The dungarees and hunched hands-in-the-pockets shoulders suggest personality of a kind. I wonder for a moment whether our daughter really found them quite as charming at the time as I did, or was it another of the unimagined traumas parents inflict with the very best of intentions on their children.

The skills in the knitting are obvious. The dolls all appear to be the work of one creator. Their faces are almost identical and each doll is about 20 centimetres tall. They are dressed in work clothes or traditional costume, and for the last quarter of a century they've been stashed away with much of the comfort-confection that furnished Lucy's childhood, in a box in an attic in a house in the Scottish Highlands, waiting perhaps for a reincarnation, a second coming, so far from Skattungbyn, the little settlement on the edge of a pine valley where brown bears still roam wild and who knows who is driving through in that nondescript old car.

# 40

## skiv *slice*

ʃiːv

Beware of false friends. In language teaching, the concept of 'false friends' describes words in one language that look or sound the same and appear to mean the same thing in another one but actually have a different and often unhelpful meaning in the second language. In one of the first lessons I ever taught in Sweden, I handed out British newspapers and asked students to find something interesting to tell the class.

When it was seventy-five-year-old Ola's turn, he looked slowly around the room, entirely without irony, and announced in sonorous tones, 'I have found a lovely picture of Princess Margaret on my backside.'

Nothing kills a joke like explaining it. The Swedish word *baksidan* means 'back page'. A false friend.

Then there are the words in a new language you confuse or make assumptions about. *Skiv* is 'slice'. *Att skiva* is 'to slice'. *Skiva* (plural *skivor*) is a disc, a record. For me, they fused and (erroneously) became the same word. How poetic, I thought, that Swedish called records 'slices'.

The first joke I understood in Swedish was about *skivor*, the slices not the records. There was a Swedish Bread Institute, and in the 1970s they ran a campaign to encourage Swedes to eat more of it, screening cinema adverts in which two old-timers sit and talk about how they've heard you're supposed to eat *sex till åtta skivor bröd om dagen*, six to eight slices of bread per day.

Swedish numbers and pronunciation are sometimes quite similar to English, where for example if you say 'six to eight' quickly it can sound like 'sixty-eight'. In Swedish, too. Imagine the shock on the old-timer's face, therefore, when he hears his friend tell him that the *Socialstyrelesen*, National Board of Health and Welfare, is supporting the campaign to get you to eat *sextiåtta skivor bröd om dagen*, sixty-eight slices of bread per day!

Well, I laughed.

It was a laugh of recognition, perhaps of relief; a threshold had been crossed. I might never be able to tell a joke in Swedish but I could now understand one. And it was a brilliant advertising campaign, still remembered with a smile by Swedes of that generation, fifty years on. I think of it now and hear that language and feel it, making the shapes and sounds I like to make with my mouth. I hear the booming sound in the auditorium's half-dark, and I feel a shiver, standing outside Sandrews cinema in Kungsgatan, waiting for my girlfriend to appear from the *tunnelbana* station at Hötorget, Haymarket, laughing into the rain.

# Part 5

On 27 April 1976, my Tuesday morning class met for the last time. The spring term was coming to an end and I was about to return to England, unsure quite why.

I had lived in Sweden longer than I had been at university, and although I could not have articulated it then, some part of my deep subconscious knew that a template had been steadily cut over almost four years for a better life than I could ever have understood had I not applied for that one job on that one occasion I consulted that one page of the *Times Educational Supplement*. Even now, writing that, the power of it and the thought of how easily I might have missed it has raised my heart rate, constricted my throat, giddied me.

I'm sure of the date, because back then I had a habit of writing my name, the date and the place where I bought it in every book I acquired, and there it is in my half-a-century-ago handwriting, in the treasured copy of *Stockholmsbilder*, 'Pictures of Stockholm': 'Stephen R. Keeler, April 27th 1976, Farewell gift from Skeppargatan Tuesday morning class'. And here, tucked between the pages of the book, is the card they all signed – Ella and Asta; Birgitta, Maja and Stig; Martin, Kristina and Carmen, and Marianne who wrote the message: *Dear Stephen, We will express our heartily thanks for your very interesting instruction in the Spring of 1976. Some of your pupils had the pleasure to be educated two years ago. We shall miss you badly and we wish you good luck for the future.*

*We hope meeting you again. Yours sincerely...* and there are nine gold star stickers, one next to each student's name.

Was it Asta who had owned a dress shop in *Gamla Stan*, the Old Town, and Ella with the troublesome Alfa Romeo? Was it Carmen who brought cakes to every lesson and Kristina who brought her divorce? And, as ever, why do I not remember either of the two men?

Skeppargatan is one in a grid of streets of sturdy, earnestly handsome nineteenth-century apartment houses that make up the affluent Östermalm quarter overlooking the inner-city Baltic quayside where sedate steamers still sail out to the archipelago. Our purpose-built classroom was on the ground floor of one of these apartment houses, near the junction with Storgatan and normally a five-minute walk from Östermalmstorg *tunnelbana*, underground, station. Lateness is not easily tolerated or readily forgiven in Sweden, and on this of all days, for our last lesson, I needed to be at best early, at worst on time.

As I hope I've already established, this was a time of great, rapid and progressive change in Stockholm. Glass and steel and concrete were replacing bricks and stucco and carved stone; birchwood replaced ornate plasterwork; geometry began to take over from the organic. A new Scandinavian style was emerging out of the old Baltic one, as Sweden began to look less towards eastern Europe and to draw more from its own design heritage. It was a time of redevelopment and refurbishment, and for a long while it felt as though every apartment house in the city had just been, was being or was about to be renovated. Tenants were relocated, buildings gutted, apartments refitted. Elevators were installed where the architecture allowed, and scaffolding rose from every street pavement as facades were sandblasted and re-rendered. Parking bays were suspended and contractors' skips occupied the roadsides, filled and refilled with rubble, great splinters of timber, old toilets and washbasins and an occasional and often exquisite *kakelugn*, tiled stove, no longer fashionable or of practical use.

As I marched briskly up the hill to my last lesson with the Skeppargatan Tuesday morning class, I must have walked under half a dozen scaffolding tunnels and side-stepped a dozen skips. It was a bright spring day, but it was plaster dust not pollen that hung in the air. There would be Carmen's cakes, stomach-churning boiled coffee, probably a nervous speech and a 'surprise' end-of-course present for the teacher, me. And then they would go home, like a small circus leaving town, to their suburban villas and inner-city apartments, to husbands and children, and one or two to empty rooms, dusty with memories, souvenirs and old books.

I was a block away when, stepping off the pavement to let a line of schoolchildren pass, I spotted a photograph album lying within reach among the rubble and smashed plasterboard in a skip. It never occurred to me not to take it.

As the children passed I blew brick dust off the album and brushed away loose plaster to reveal a lovely tooled leather family album tied with a plaited thong with intricately knotted tassels. That it was very old was clear. The leather was stiff, and cracked in places. The black pages were thick as board. The photographs were held with tiny, gold-lined black photo corners, and each was captioned in what might at one time have been white fountain-pen ink, now turned semi-visible, caramelised orange, in a free-flowing but disciplined hand-lettered copperplate script: Bertil, Claes, Charlotte, Emil, Alice...

How long I stood in the street, carefully turning the pages, entranced by what I was looking at, I'm not sure, but I was suddenly late. I stuffed the album into my briefcase and began to jog up the road to my class, arriving hot and apologetic but with a ready-made excuse, and one of the best lessons we ever had, in my bag.

The abandoned lesson plan lay on the desk. I took out the album and held it up, explaining where I'd found it.

There were twenty or so stiff pages. Each held no more than four photographs. Most were black-and-white, taken outdoors and remarkably sharp. A few were studio shots in frayed and fading sepia. All had been taken before or during the First World War and showed the same large and obviously wealthy family in front of fine Strandvägen houses or in the former royal park of Djurgården nearby.

The same characters appeared again and again. And they *were* characters, like something out of Strindberg or Ibsen, or even Chekhov. There were louche young men in pince-nez, with unfeasible moustaches and striped blazers, sporting whites and the soft caps worn then for cycling There were young women in enormous skirts and billowing blouses, hair piled high, collars tightly buttoned, some of them holding long-handled wooden tennis rackets. There were children in sailor suits, and there was a small family spaniel. It was like a catalogue of costume design references for *Fanny and Alexander*.

One group photograph held our attention longest – for by now my students had crowded around the album, recognising streets and buildings and calling out gleefully how they had been photographed there or there or there as children themselves. It was winter, great trees drooped under a weight of snow. Strandvägen is a thin pencil sketch in the white distance, and the newly opened Nordic Museum (1907) is nearby, like a gingerbread house gabled with icing, among fir saplings. It is a large family. The impressively tall and heavily bearded patriarch, in a splendid full-length overcoat with astrakhan collar and tall hat, fine leather gloves and (we imagined) hand-made winter shoes, stands unsmiling at the centre of the picture. His wife, similarly tall and younger than we might have assumed her to be, is arrayed like Solomon in all his glory in an exquisitely tailored winter coat, sumptuously draped with the finest of fine furs – sable and Siberian fox, we fantasised – an elegant hat with black lace half-veil, and soft leather gloves disappearing under great fur-trimmed cuffs. There were what we took to be grown-up children with their families, so grandchildren then, with sleds and skates and even a bicycle fitted with skis. There was a high-standing baby-carriage. There were snow-shoes and a pair of cross-country skis. There were, too, at either end of this tableau of winter splendour, the domestic staff, modest in their poses and their functional winter uniform coats. Two were holding muffled infants; another restrained the spaniel. In all, perhaps thirty people posing for the photographer on a day that could have been fifteen degrees below freezing, at the end of the nineteenth century. Why? What had brought the entire household and extended family out onto the ice that day for this photographic event?

Asta remembered a winter coat she'd had in the 1930s – red with black braiding, 'like a Cossack's'. Her parents had saved a year to buy it for her. Carmen had had skates exactly like those in the photo, with leather straps and silver buckles. Birgitta remembered her grandfather making ski-like blades for the back wheel of her bicycle. Maja knew the photographic studio, long gone, where the indoor photos had been taken. Marianne recalled her father's camera, etched with Victor Hasselblad's signature and pawned to pay the rent sometime in the 1930s. And on it went, this stream-of-consciousness 'lesson' of Swedish brand names and place names, of events – beginnings and endings – of rites of passage, journeys, destinations, departures and clothes, those clothes – the best of them bought from the new (1917) Nordiska Kompaniet (NK) department store. Later, the cars, the trams, the *tunnelbana*; toys and games, going to school, learning to read, the books, the stories and, of course, Pippi Longstocking; the comings together and the splittings assunder and on it went and on it would have gone had it not been for the next class of students gathering impatiently outside, waiting for us to vacate the classroom for the last lesson of the term.

I learned more Swedish social and cultural history in that hour and a half – and in the best possible way – than if I'd enrolled on a year-long diploma course. And it had come at the right time. Had I found the album in the early weeks of my first arrival in Sweden, I could not have learned so much from it or from my students, who had, in the best traditions of education, become my teachers. What we learn is in a sense what we already know. There has to be fertile ground. My fertile ground had been four years in the making, and this was just one more hugely fortuitous gift among those that this country seemed to want to keep giving me.

At the time, I gave no thought to who had made the photograph album with such evident care and skill. I didn't consider who its last owner might have been, nor why it had been abandoned to such an indignity. Had the last surviving family member lived here until a few weeks ago? Had the album been given to a faithful retainer as a parting souvenir? Would-be novelists, go ahead and see what you can make of it.

Alas, I no longer have the album in my possession.

# 41

## skog *forest*
sku:g

I had never seen so many trees. The towns of
Västergötland and the villages of the north were
literally hedged around with pine and spruce, like
bald pink patches in an animal's fur where a wound
has healed. Only in the cities, in Gothenburg and
Malmö and less so in Stockholm, was the forest
forced back enough to fade a little from the collective
consciousness.

In the 1960s and 70s, most urban Swedes had not
long come in from the cold countryside to towns and
cities that grew rapidly. Or they were perhaps second-
generation urbanites. The forest had defined their
grandparents; it defined their parents; it defined them
still, if only in memory, in the ogres and the trolls of
childhood tales. One of the first books I bought in
Sweden was of Swedish fairy tales illustrated with
the great John Bauer's paintings of the overwhelming
forest, the long tall trees, suggested murk and the
bouldersome forest floor with perhaps a toadstool
here and there. From fairy tales of childhood to the
playground and natural classroom of youth, the forest
was the most generous resource to ameliorate the
often grinding lives of adults. Every man owned a knife
and could fashion tools and toys. Every settlement had
its two-handed cross-saw, and the great chains and

horses that would pull the trees when they were felled or had to be removed.

My weekly train ride to Laxå flickered through the forest. Even I felt it like a kind of rebirth. Driving north from Stockholm, it isn't long before the forest edges closer to the roadside. The drive from Furudal to Rättvik flashed through trees like silent-movie film frames clacketting through the gate. We often late-night-speculated how 'The Bruk' might look once Lennart and his magic island in the forest had gone, the trees moving in and swallowing it whole in half a decade.

Everyone I knew lived in a wooden house. Half my students worked in forestry or the paper mill, construction or carpentry. It is hard to overstate the significance of wood and the forest in the Swedish psyche. Social invitations were to 'the forest', to jog or ski or orienteer; to pick *lingon* or, if you were honoured and trusted, to visit the secret places where the *kantareller*, chanterelle mushrooms, grew.

It was in the forest that I watched a bull elk the size of a small cottage and his mate guide their two young across the road, while a dozen cars and buses waited in wonderment. The same forest and the same road where A was killed when he hit one in his truck and the antlers went through the windscreen and his skull. The same forest where the bears came down to feed in autumn, and where in a blizzard I saw my only wolf pause to take a long look at me, before turning without reaction and trotting into the trees. It was in the forest, a day before I met her, that Yvonne had picnicked and collected the mosquito bites whose scars remained until the day she died.

# 42

## smör *butter*

smɜːr

An early-acquired word for me for its onomatopoeic qualities – the sibilant glide into the vowel, which I know I always over-lengthen when saying the word *smu … rr*. That suggestion, too, of the English word 'smear', but richer, somehow creamier, lower in the throat.

When I first met Yvonne she was living in a very smart apartment in downtown Stockholm. The landlord was a Norwegian shipping magnate whose daughter, Å, lived in the same block. Å had had polio as a child and had a live-in nurse/companion in a fully adapted apartment. She also flung a huge BMW 7-series around town with great wooden blocks on the pedals so that she could reach them, and a swivel knob on the steering wheel so that her tiny hands could handle the car with panache. One of the conditions of our low rent was that we would give Å regular English lessons. It was our good fortune that she was a lovely and often outrageously eccentric woman, great fun to be with. We spent hours with Å and her companion E, often late into the evening over fresh prawns and iced *akvavit*, and became good friends. At Easter 1975, Å invited us to Norway to stay with her family in Molde for a couple of weeks.

The butter at breakfast each morning was served by
her adorable mother, in a porcelain dish decorated
with stylised paintings that I always took to be two
Norwegian children, one with a school bag, the other
with two baguettes under her arm. In a curling hand-
written style was printed the motto, in Norwegian:
*Smör og bröd gjör kinden röd*: loose translation, 'Bread
and butter gives you rosy cheeks.'

I must have enthused so much about this lovely butter
dish that they gave it to us on our departure back to
Stockholm. I have it still, here in front of me now, and
until today, wanting to double-check my translation,
I had always (i.e. for half a century) read the motto
as *Smör og bröd gjör kinder röd*, that is to say, 'Bread
and butter makes children healthy' – a not implausible
error. I'm glad I'm finally able to correct it, and in doing
so discover a related Swedish saying that I hadn't
come across before: *Ost*, cheese, *och bröd gör kinden
röd*, 'Bread and cheese gives you rosy cheeks.'

# 43

# smörgåsbord *smorgasbord*

sмɜːrgɔs'buːrd

You grow protective of your words of love; you take possession of them like the billet doux of youth, returned or rediscovered in old age. Their perceived misuse by others seems disrespectful, and you wince at mispronunciations, you become intolerant of casual misappropriation.

The *smörgåsbord* is the smell and taste of Swedish love spread far and wide, from five-star Emirates hotels to every Scandi-themed restaurant across the globe, from Melbourne to Majorca. It is fine dining at the Opera in Stockholm, and it is every bourgeois family's Christmas treat at a restaurant they maybe visit only annually for that purpose. For me, the *smörgåsbord* will always be a meal at sea.

There used to be great ferries between Scandinavia and Britain. When I first lived in Sweden in 1973, flying there would have been unthinkable. Only the rich and famous and business folk flew, and had we thought about it at all we'd have been grateful for the low-priced rolling luxury offered by the Tor Line ferries from Immingham and Felixstowe to Gothenburg, three times a week.

I made over seventy crossings on the old *Tor Anglia* and *Tor Hollandia* and later on the swanky new *Tor*

*Scandinavia* and *Tor Britannia*, which were given brief low-budget fame in the TV series *Triangle* made on board. I crossed in winter storms so fierce they had to drop the anchor and ride it out, and in midsummer calms so still the ships seemed not move.

As always, it is the first time I remember most vividly. I had just come out of hospital in Stockholm after a minor operation, and was fragile and bandaged. My girlfriend had made the bookings, which included the long-distance bus from Stockholm to the ferry terminal in Gothenburg. It was winter. I was cold. I never had the right clothes. Sitting was painful and I felt nauseous the whole way.

The bus was delayed long enough for us to spend the last couple of hours of the journey convinced we were going to miss the ferry. In fact we arrived an hour after its scheduled departure time to find it hadn't sailed because of bad weather out at sea. Had I felt well enough, I'd have worried about that. Glad to be on board, I found my cheap couchette – a kind of bunk bed on an open corridor so far below deck that the floor pointed downwards. I didn't care. I slept. The ferry must have departed, for I remember being thrown from my bunk as it rolled on the highest of high seas – this was one of those anchor-dropping crossings.

I remembered the advice from Erik, who had been a cook in the Swedish merchant navy: plenty of dry crispbread, as much *Ramlösa*, a Swedish brand of mineral water, as you can drink, and stand out on deck looking at the horizon. So there I was, shivering in the dark, not entirely dry, gripping the deck rail with every ounce of strength I still had and forcing crispbread and mineral water down me while trying to keep my eyes on some imagined out-there horizon. And it worked. I have never been seasick.

Next morning I was the only passenger in the dining room piling my plate high with what would have been last night's *smörgåsbord* had the sea been calm enough to allow it to be served. Not the classic way to experience your first one, but as the ship continued to buck and shudder and roll and dip, and crockery flew across the room, chased by stewards trying not to look alarmed, I held onto my chair and to the plates around me and felt myself healing with each mouthful of Baltic herring in mustard sauce, and every slice of spiced ham. The rolls were fresh, the butter salty, the coffee dark and strong. The predominantly Danish crew, perhaps impressed that I had managed to turn up for 'breakfast' when no one else had, offered me *akvavit*, alcoholic spirit, and I drank it, neat. And chased it with *stor stark*, a large, strong beer. It was eight in the morning. Of course it was like falling in love: I was falling in love.

Over the years, on every subsequent crossing and long after Tor Line had been swallowed up by DFDS Danish Seaways, we always booked a table for the evening *smörgåsbord* and always rose to the grandeur of its many etiquettes. We took a sauna first and always dressed for dinner: a meal that never failed to satisfy, even if none was ever quite as memorable as that storm-tossed first.

44

___

## snö *snow*

sn3:

It is early February and the snow is drifting in my corner of the north-west Scottish Highlands. Something reminiscent about watching fat flakes soft-landing, accruing, and I recall the shuffled thrill if it snowed while we were penned in our County Durham primary school classrooms – a lighter grey, ragged across a darker sky – and how our parents and grandparents hated it. As if their quotidian lives weren't grinding enough.

The only fun to be had in snow, it seemed, was on the covers of comics and annuals, where rosy-cheeked children from a happy land, in long scarves and bright wellies, built unfeasible snowmen, and slid and skated and sledged with abandon and without mishap towards smiling dads and jumping spaniels. It was the merciful stuff of the Ladybird Books that brought much of the joy and most of the colour into my early years.

Imagine my confusion, that first winter in Mariestad, when the handsome town became an exquisite wood engraving overnight. Winter tyres were mandatory so traffic didn't slither to a precarious standstill. Everyone had the necessary kit, and that made going out not only possible but a thrill. I have a sudden flashback to the Teddy Boys who gathered like huddled crows by the public lavatories on the High Row in Darlington, in their polyester jackets and drainpipe jeans, summer and winter; pinched and hunched and spivved up for nothing.

It is not by chance that the Orrefors crystal 'Snowball' has become a Swedish design classic. It can only be chance that it was designed (by Ann Wärff) and introduced in the year I arrived in Mariestad, 1973.

The first time I saw what must surely have inspired its design was during my first winter living in Stockholm. I taught an evening class on Lidingö – a wealthy, bourgeois island suburb of the city – and had to travel by *tunnelbana* and bus to get there. It was a further ten-minute walk along an elegant avenue of picture-book villas and Carl Larsson gardens to my classroom.

That evening the snow was half a metre deep, crusted and glistering at minus fifteen Celsius. I trudged in the dark between feeble pools of pale yellow street-light, watching my footing and trying not to shiver. And there, close to my feet as I almost passed it unseeing, was a pyramid of snowballs by the mailbox of 'Familjen Carlsson'. Each ball was the size of a *semla* and they'd been stacked with some skill, and in the space created inside the pyramid was a stub of flickering candle, lighting the structure from within. What joy! I stopped and looked up. There was another, and another, and another, at maybe five-metre intervals, all the way along the curving path to the steps of the front porch and the Carlsson family's handsome front door.

The sky was black and, yes, perforated with pin-prick stars; the night was as still as any night I've known. Not a sound. I stood and looked, and quite possibly my mouth fell open.

## 45

# tåg *train*
tɔːg

I had my fifteen minutes of fame in the 1980s, with a small but bestselling book of listening skills practice exercises for students of English as a Foreign Language. Long out of print now, it paid our mortgage then.

There was a student book and a cassette to accompany it. Several 'chapters' used recorded public service announcements ('At the airport', 'On the train', and such-like), and I begin to understand now that they must have come out of my earliest encounters with Swedish.

'*Se upp för dörrarna!*', 'Mind the doors!', and '*Dörrarna stängs*', 'Doors closing', are the first phrases I heard on the Stockholm *tunnelbana*, and so I began to acquire an embryonic grasp of how plurals are formed, the definite article and aspects of the passive voice.

'*Tåget mot Stockholm kommer strax in på spår ett*', 'the train to Stockholm will soon arrive at platform one', has stayed with me these fifty years.

*Tåg* – something I love about pronouncing it, the tongue touching the back of the upper teeth, the long, low vowel – it helps if you're a northerner – and the soft-landing 'g'. And *strax*, soon – a bit like sex, something I somehow knew before I was taught it.

Not everything was instinctive. It took me far too long to work out that *Nyapåstigningar* – unlike the towns of Nyköping and Nynäshamn, for example – was not the next station we would arrive at but rather what the ticket inspector calls out, '*Nya påstigningar*', literally, newly boarded, when passing through the train after each stop.

*Tåg* then, a word with a friendly aspect. Like the Little Blue Engine in the stories by Ursula Hourihane read to me by my great-grandmother, as embers collapsed in the grate and the wind-up clock on her sideboard struggled to chime the quarter-hours, long, long before I could read for myself. *Tåg* – the little yellow railbus waddling through the forest, back in time to a gentler, quieter place.

# 46

## **toalet** *toilet*

tʊʌ'let

The Swedish royal family has Napoleonic origins, and there are still traces of the French connection, not least in the language. Most European languages borrowed from French during the eighteenth and nineteenth centuries. It was chic to do so, and French often had words for concepts that were new in other cultures.

I like what Swedish did with its French loot: it tweaked the pronunciations here and there and dressed the immigrants in Swedish motley. Thus the French *toilette*, toilet, was given half an extra syllable and in Swedish looks like this: *toalet*.

English never adopted the French *trottoir*, pavement, footpath, but Swedish did, and made it look a little less effete: *trottoar*. *Toalet*, a word I use, and *trottoar*, one I can never remember having uttered in conversation, are words for love in Swedish. What pleasure, rolling them around my mouth like a Swiss chocolate.

Another is *byrå*, office – that 'y', pronounced by shaping the mouth for 'oo' and then saying 'ee'. I never took to *fauteuil*, armchair, in French, so the Swedish *fåtölj* leaves me cold. But I don't mind waiting in an occasional *kö*, queue, and it was in Sweden, before Greta Thunberg's parents had started school, that I learned about concern for the *miljö*, environment.

# 47

## **trana** *crane*

'trɑːnʌ

I began to dream in the culture that was, although I didn't yet know it, starting to adopt me. Some events take on a dreamlike quality even as they happen, leaving lifelong questions and vagueness only the dead could have answered.

That year (1973-4) in Mariestad now seems like a magic realism episode in a novel I'm not sure I even read. Did I really drive around for a year in a cream Ford Mustang, loaned to me by a generous and quietly spoken student, S, who mentioned almost in passing as I pulled away from my first traffic lights on the test drive before he handed it over, '... hm ... Stephen ... in Sweden ... we drive ... on the right ...'? Have I imagined another of my students, A, always carrying a loaded pistol in her handbag in case her crippling depressions suddenly overwhelmed her? And did I allow myself to be transported across the vastness of Lake Vänern, unable to swim and without a life jacket, in a miniature but perhaps appropriately named 'Optimist' class yacht, by the eleven-year-old son of my then landlady – in the dark, in October?

The cranes of Lake Hornborga are one of my most dreamlike memories from that time. It was 1975 and I was living in Stockholm and working for (try to say this) Kursverksamheten vid Stockholms Universitetet (fourteen syllables, spoken as one word if you can do it). I had a four-weekend consultancy at the Volvo engine plant at Trollhättan, 'The Troll's Hat'. Was ever a town better named for an episode of magic realism? So each Friday evening for four weeks I took the train down to Hjo, a pretty lakeside town where there was a gleaming Volvo saloon waiting for me at the station with the keys in the exhaust pipe. Did that even happen? I drove to the serene lakeside hotel and emptied the minibar before steak and chips, a black-and-white episode of 'The Brothers' *'Arvingarna'* – 'The Heirs' on Swedish telly – and an early night.

Next morning I would meet my four Volvo executives and we'd spend the next forty-eight hours 'doing' what was then called Intensive Business English, before I returned to Stockholm on the late-night Sunday train.

The first three weekends had gone well enough. We got on, they worked hard and made discernible progress, and there was a factory visit where I watched robots build the engine I got to start for its first time. But there was a restraint I found unsatisfactory, as though I wasn't fully engaging these four thoroughly decent, hard-working and utterly committed middle managers. My having taken, inexplicably, to wearing fat velvet bow-ties and a deerstalker hat almost certainly didn't help break the ice.

For the final weekend, they suggested we leave the classroom and instead take a trip to nearby Lake Hornborga 'to see the cranes dance'. Another high-end Volvo; another pleasant drive on sturdy, traffic-free roads through a Swedish spring waking from the long brown winter; another dream...

The cranes have been stopping off to feed on the vodka potatoes in the damp fields around Lake Hornborga, on their annual spring migration, for as long as there have been potato fields to feed in. They are fantastical, silk-embroidered birds. In my poem 'At Lake Hornborga Watching Cranes', I liken them to 'an archduke's hat with pins'. They bounce on sprung-steel legs as thin as wire, and when they 'dance' it is as though everything around them unfocuses. You cannot turn away.

I had discarded the bow-tie and ridiculous hat for a leather jacket and sturdy shoes. A good move. I must have looked like a fellow human being to my students for the first time. One of them lent me his binoculars. We walked a short distance through last summer's long-dead long grass and then stopped to watch.

Someone took a photograph from behind. I have it here. I am standing, holding the binoculars to my eyes, unaware of land or sky or anyone nearby or far away. It is as though I too had feathers, the heft of the birds, the lightness of being, the air, the lift, the half-flight mating dance of the cranes at Lake Hornborga.

## 48
___

### träskor *clogs*
'træ'skuːr

I was taught, in the well-meaning but distantly puzzled and self-satisfied way that facts about foreigners were presented in British schools, that Dutch people wore clogs. By extension, I grew to believe that only Dutch people wore clogs, and probably only Dutch tulip-farmers and cheese-makers.

My characteristic grammar school arrogance sat astride a yawning chasm of ignorance fortified with such self-belief that I was frequently outraged to discover a new or opposing truth. Such as that Swedes wore clogs, that clogs were a part of traditional Swedish agrarian culture, and that far from being cute or touristy, they were still bought and worn all over Sweden.

*Träskor*, clogs, is another of my much-loved Swedish literalisms. The Swedish word for shoes is *skor*. *Trä*, wood, sounds so much like the English word 'tree' that my mind's-eye image of *träskor* is of 'tree-shoes', for which I owe a debt of thanks to Mr H, my French master in the lower fourth, whose teaching methodology comprised the twin strategies of corporal punishment and literal translation. Thus, a sentence such as 'My sister surpassed herself in her school exams' was rendered, under Mr H's method, as 'My sister – *ma soeur* – slap-on-the-head – she is surpassed herself

– *s'est surpassée* – slap-on-the-head – in – *dans* – slap – her examinations of the school – *ses examinations d'école* – slap, slap, slap.'

It came as no surprise to discover that Mr H had learned his French as a prisoner of war.

I have my 'tree-shoes' by the back door, ready for outdoor wear, and long ago discovered I can drive in them. Probably not a good idea: when I turned up for my first-ever flying lesson wearing a brand new pair, my instructor made me leave them on the tarmac and fly barefoot. Something about the possibility of them slipping off and getting stuck in the pedals.

Our unsophisticated schoolboy revenge on Mr H? The soubriquet we gave him. Bald as a billiard ball, he was forever known as *oeuf-tête*. I know, I know: it should have been *tête d'oeuf*, head of egg, slap.

## 49

# **varsågod** *you're welcome, etc*
'vʌʃɒ'guːd

Students of the language are famously taught early on that Swedish has no word for 'please'. How rude! And how wrong.

The word most often used for 'please' in Swedish is 'thank you', *tack*. So the answer to 'Would you like..?' questions is most often *'ja tack'*, 'yes, thank you'. There are numerous other words for 'please' when you want to be particularly formal, 'Would you please?', or when you want to literally plead. It is an example of where a language has no single one-to-one corresponding word for the same concept in most other languages.

The opposite is also found in Swedish. *Varsågod* has a huge variety of meanings depending on the context in which it's used.  Because I *acquired* the little Swedish I know by living in Sweden, rather than learning it from books and in classrooms, I had and have no difficulty knowing instinctively, the way I know much English usage, when to employ it to mean, for example:

– You're welcome, after someone has thanked you, somewhat in the way *'prego'* is used in Italian.

– Come in, when welcoming someone into your home.

– Please, sit down/take a seat

– Please have this, when offering food, drink, sweets, anything in fact.

– This way, when showing someone where to go.

– Yes, of course, when someone excuses themselves to get past you.

*Varsågod*, literally means 'be', var-, 'so', -så-, 'good', -god), and after *hej*, hello, and *tack*, thank you, it is probably the most useful word to get to know early.

It was a word we took home with us, along with our cheese slices and Orrefors crystal 'Snowball' candleholders, when we left Sweden – we thought – for good. It became woven into our family's ideolect once we were back in the UK. Our daughter grew up hearing it, and we could use it more widely when we had Swedish friends to stay or when British friends who'd worked with us in Sweden came to visit. It is a word which is so deep-rooted in me it has extended beyond being a mere lexical item. It carries significance. It is a signifier, another signifier, of my organic coming together with Sweden and its people and culture.

If I were ever invited to make a donation to the BBC Radio 4 'Museum of Curiosity', it would be the Swedish word *varsågod*.

## 50

**vitsippa** *wood anemone*

'viːt'sɪpʌ

> Daisies are our silver,
> Buttercups our gold:
> This is all the treasure
> We can have or hold.

> *Jan Struther (1901-1953)*

No idea how many times I must have sung this, drowned out by Miss Swift's heavy foot on the sustain pedal of the school hall upright, throughout the 1950s. It is a sweet children's hymn made sweeter for me in old age by its clear appeal for temperance and humility. It is, I see it now, a socialist hymn, advocating qualities I was to discover were embedded in the Swedes' social democratic construct of *lagom*.

What Miss Swift offered us in music and religion-lite, Mrs Ransome showed us in pictures and on Nature Study walks. Only the supremely indifferent or those inured by deprivation or abuse could have come out of that primary education ignorant of all the birds' names and the wildflowers, or unable to tell an elm from an ash. In support, there were the profoundly formative paintings of Charles F Tunnicliffe, whose illustrations for the Ladybird Books *What to Look For in...* series and for Brooke Bond Tea cards were the backdrop, wings and stage set I chose for my otherwise grim, industrial environment.

My daughter and I spent a Swedish *Midsommar* with good friends a few years ago and took to out-distancing each other on our morning runs along Lake Siljan. In describing the point at which she had turned off the forest track and headed for the lakeside path on a new run, she said: 'You'll easily find it, dad. There's yellow flag growing, a coot's nest and some reeds, set out just like a Tunnicliffe.' I found it and she was right. It was like an illustration from *What to Look For in Spring*. Mrs Ransome, your work was not in vain.

So, I knew water avens and speedwell, loved red campion and herb robert, and could tell coltsfoot from dandelion at fifty paces, but these flowers were increasingly hard to find – had to be sought out now – in the Britain I was leaving. Which helps explain the impact on me of Swedish wildflower meadows.

The road between Rättvik and Mora, around the northern shore of Lake Siljan, is calendar-beautiful. It passes villages of red-painted cottages, each with its white flagpole; it plunges into tall forests of shattering light; and it skirts meadows on either side that bubble with cowslips and yawn bright yellow with buttercups. Spring is my favourite time of year for that drive, for that is when great swathes of the forest floor are spilled over with *vitsippor*, wood anemones, and the rarer *blåsippor*, hepatica. It is as though the ancient forest itself is shifting in a wakening, calling out for fresh linen, crisp, white, renewed.

The first present Yvonne gave me was a tiny bunch of grape hyacinths so blue it almost hurt the eyes to look. I had a dark apartment with a galley kitchen on Kocksgatan, on *Södermalm*, Stockholm's south island, and this was her first visit. I cooked *Poulet Marengo* from Katharine Whitehorn's *Cooking in a Bedsitter*, and she brought the flowers from the florist on the corner of my street.

There was a fashion in Sweden in those days for sprigs of flowers arranged as Tunnicliffe might have arranged them and set in blocks of clear acrylic. Something about them, both sharp and modern and at the same time funereal and Victorian, appealed to me the first time I saw one in a florist's window. I have it here, the one I bought for Yvonne a few months after the grape hyacinths and Chicken Marengo. It fits neatly into my palm and holds three *vitsippor*, forever young but clearly ageing: caught like a studio portrait, intended to remind, to transmit forever the loving impulse that made me buy it that sunny early morning at the little florist's on the corner of Birger Jarlsgatan and Hamngatan, and now at home on the slate windowsill of my Scottish bedroom, the first thing I see on waking, every day.

# Epilogue

Throughout a lifetime, it is not just people who come and go, like extras in a movie. Objects, too, play seminal if sometimes apparently peripheral roles in our lives. The album might have been thrown out the day before or the day after I passed the skip. Had I not had to pause to let children go by, I might never have seen it. That book, that crystal vase, that porcelain figure you disliked at first, those matching silver photo frames; the certificates, receipts, newspaper cuttings, old driving licences and medical cards: these are the coincidental things that lives are made of. The Russian poet Maria Stepanova has written authoritatively on the workings of memory. The quotation from her magnum opus that I have used as an epigraph to this book was intended to set the tone as well as the scene for what you have, I hope, just read.

The things that my life has been made of have turned out to be mostly Swedish. Of course, there were the Meccano and Dinky Toys of my 1950s north of England childhood, the snake-clasp belts and Clarks shoes, the 1960s singles and my first car in the 1970s, a dismal Triumph Herald coupé. But I had said goodbye to all that. This book turns out to have been a lot about serendipity. I put it like that because writers don't always know what it is they're going to write about until it's there on the page in front of them. We are the first to read our thoughts. When I decided to write this love letter to Sweden, I did not imagine that so many of my fifty words would be for or closely associated with food. Perhaps there is some truth left in the old cliché that the way to a man's heart is through his stomach. In the 1970s, you didn't go to Sweden for the food. That, like so much in the country, has changed since I first arrived there.

Now I know a little better what the book is about, I also know a little better what I think of the things that it is about. But new questions arise that I had not much considered before. Why was I so determined to leave Britain? Why, especially given my background, had I been so open to this particular opportunity and all the others it made possible? And still today, how to explain the power and the depth of the love that grew for this place? Has it all been nothing more than exquisite and charming coincidence?

*Lagom*, before we go?

Moderate, just right, not too much and not too little is what the dictionaries will offer. But *lagom* represents more than can be translated word-for-word. Philosophy is perhaps too grand. Way of behaving, way of thinking, way of perceiving the world, maybe.

I have a number of wealthy Swedish friends. None of them lives in a gated development, none has a swimming pool, none drives a high performance car; they don't stay in swanky hotels and their houses are not showrooms of excess; they don't wear hand-made shoes or eat in Michelin-starred restaurants. All could afford it but none would risk the outward show of wealth. None would want their neighbours or their friends to think they thought so highly of themselves. Their way, their lifestyle is like the temperature inside their homes, *lagom*. There used to be a butter-substitute spread in Sweden called *Lätt och Lagom*, and perhaps a decent if loose translation of that would be 'light and right'. Swedish society has changed enormously since I first arrived at Arlanda Airport on a rainy August afternoon in 1973. *Lagom* – moderation in all things – may not have the power it once had to shape behaviour, but it still exerts a social force to curb extravagance and limit excess. The word was never one of my fifty words for love in Swedish, but the concept it signifies appealed then and still charms me today.

I have arrived at that moment writers dream of, the moment when I can type 'The End' on the last page. And when I do that, I shall go downstairs and butter a couple of bits of Leksands *knäckebröd*. I shall take two or three slivers of *gravad lax* from the fridge and place them on the crispbread, then drop a little dill sauce onto each. I'll pour myself a shot of iced Skåne *akvavit* in one of the beautiful hand-blown 'Viking' glasses my dear old friends Birgitta and John sent as a Christmas present nearly thirty years ago, and I shall raise that glass to you, my reader, and drink the *snaps*, small shot of neat spirit, in one, having saluted you in the only way appropriate at the end of our Swedish jaunt together, with thanks and to your very good health: '*Skål!*'

Stephen Keeler
Ullapool, Stockholm and Siljansäs
2021

# Acknowledgements

In addition to being dedicated to my lovely late wife, Yvonne, who was British but whom I met in Stockholm in 1974, this book is for the many Swedes who welcomed me, and later my wife and our daughter, to their wonderful country over very many years.

None of it would have happened without Michael Lewis and Ann-Marie Lundberg of the old British Centre and Kursverksamheten vid Stockholmsuniversitetet, but my deepest thanks go to Lennart and Inger Öhnell, to whom I was introduced by Kate Mulvey.

I can think of no one to whom I owe more than I do to Lennart Öhnell, for friendship and the golden years at Furudals Bruks Kursinternat. Through him I met some of those who have become my closest friends, Birgitta Dalin (who originated the phonetic transcriptions) and John Lövgren in particular. But others should be mentioned here by name: Ann-Elise Ljungman, Ola Bertilsson, Barbro Carnehag, Marianne Sahlberg and Charlie and Kerstin Annell.

There are very many more to whom I owe so much. If it's possible to thank a country, then I thank Sweden most profoundly. I literally cannot imagine how life might have been without you.

The manuscript for *Fifty Words for Love in Swedish* was received with such generous enthusiasm, and subsequently handled with such obvious understanding and professional commitment and care by my editor, Kylie Fitzpatrick, and my designer, Michael Phillips – both of Archetype Books – that the finished book is exactly the book I wanted it to be – only a little better. Profound thanks to both.

# About the author

Stephen Keeler was born in the north-east of England in 1951. He first moved to Sweden, aged 22, as a teacher. With degrees and teaching qualifications from the universities of Durham, Leeds and London and the Royal Society of Arts, he spent almost forty years in international language education, living and working additionally in China, Vietnam, the former Yugoslavia and most of the former Soviet bloc republics of eastern Europe, as well as for the British Council, the United Nations and the BBC World Service, among others.

He commuted between London and central Sweden for almost twenty years. Now retired from full-time teaching, he studies Swedish poetry and culture and still makes frequent visits there.

Widowed in 2003, in 2010 he moved from London to the north-west Highlands of Scotland, where he writes poetry and teaches creative writing.

**Puss och kram**